WATERTIGHT MARKETING

DELIVERING LONG-TERM SALES RESULTS

BRYONY THOMAS

Watertight Marketing

First published in 2013 by

Anoma Press Ltd
48 St Vincent Drive, St Albans, Herts, AL1 5SJ, UK
info@anomapress.com
www.anomapress.com

Book layout by Neil Coe.
Cartoons by Simon Ellinas.
Editorial illustrations by Lizzie Everard.
VA-Voom! logo by Andy Fuller.

Printed on acid-free paper from managed forests. This book is printed on
demand to fulfill orders, so no copies will be remaindered or pulped.

ISBN 978-1-908746-34-4

For Eleni, whose arrival gave pause, perspective and purpose.

What other entrepreneurs have said...

"This is a breakthrough marketing book for small businesses. It ditches all the fluff and nonsense and gives a business owner exactly what they need to get their marketing in gear. You'll want to read it with a pen in hand because you will have ideas to put into action on every single page."

Mark Mason, CEO, Mubaloo

"Watertight Marketing is brilliant. Bryony has delivered a book that is free of jargon and a compelling read that makes you sit up and quickly realise where the holes are in your plans, the potential cost of these holes to your business and ultimately how to fill them and ensure your business is robust and successful."

Nick Dean, Managing Director, Ad Lib Recruitment

"**Any business who is serious about growing needs to read this book**. No clap-trap. No padding. It is chocker-block full of great ways to fix your business development processes, systems, copy, plans and activities so you stop leaking profit and see your business grow – the watertight way. As a result of reading this book, I was able to clearly identify why our own business growth has plateaued, and because of the common sense contained in the book will be working to fix that."

**Heather Townsend, author of
'The FT Guide To Business Networking' and co-author of
'How to make partner and still have a life'**

"If you're running a small business and think your marketing activity is as good as it can be, read this book. If you think your marketing could be better, read it twice. I've read many books on marketing and got a lot of value from each of them, but this is the one we will be buying to give to each of our clients. **No-nonsense wisdom, perfectly pitched to resonate with all small business owners**."

Stephen King, Managing Director, F-works

WHO ARE YOU?

If you're the owner of a small business, this book is for you. If you're a highly ambitious owner of a small business heading towards being a big business, or your goal is to build a business that sells for millions, this book is a must.

More step up than start up

There are lots of books about starting a business. There aren't so many about staying in business. And, even fewer that really show you how to step things up.

To get the most from this book, you'll already be up and running, and making money. You'll be pretty clear about what you're selling and to whom. Now, you want to scale it. You want to get better rewards for the effort you put in. You're at that stage where you need to start 'doing things properly' in order to grow.

It will give you the marketing judgement to make sure that you're always lucky on the sales front.

With marketing, this means you've tried a few things. Some will have worked, some will have failed. Often more by luck than judgement. Watertight Marketing will turn that on its head. It will give you the marketing judgement to make sure that you're always lucky on the sales front.

A totally missable marketing opportunity

This book is your shield against the never-ending onslaught of 'unmissable' marketing opportunities, designed to protect you against fruitlessly spending vast sums on activities that won't net a bean in revenue. It equips you to put a powerful marketing operation in place that really delivers for your business. That is, marketing that delivers real sales results. In the long term.

It is often in the marketing or sales guru's interest to convince you that they are the practitioner of some sort of dark art, and that you need to spend a fortune (with them) to do it. Indeed, a quick Internet search on "lead generation" will return a list of potential suppliers suggesting that a business should invest in: telesales 'guaranteed to secure appointments'; direct mail so targeted that people are practically waiting to give you their money; 'one time only' advertising deals; search engine optimisation to secure your position at the top of Google's listings; social media that can seemingly replace your whole marketing team; online word of mouth that does your selling for you... the list goes on, and on.

Given the flood of advice, it's no surprise that many businesses, large and small, suffer from Tactic Burn; that is, jumping from one 'essential' sales and marketing activity to another, never getting the consistent results that the business so badly needs. Watertight Marketing is what's missing from this picture. Without it, many businesses are stuck on the yo-yo diet of the marketing world, pursued in the hope that one day they will uncover that magic silver bullet.

Many businesses are stuck on the yo-yo diet of the marketing world, pursued in the hope that one day they will uncover that magic silver bullet.

What you need to know is that there isn't one.

There are three!

Your Bucket, your Funnels and your Taps.

Contents

Acknowledgments

Writing this bit has been the image I've held in mind when putting words on a page was the last thing I wanted to do. Because, putting these words on this page is truly wonderful. Whilst at times writing this book has felt a lonely journey, in reality I have so many people to thank...

Let me start by thanking my wonderful husband, Tom, without whom so many of my dreams would not have been fulfilled. His curiosity of mind and quiet determination has been just what's needed to keep the show on the road. Thank you.

With more direct impact on the book itself, I'd like to thank Heather Townsend for making me believe it was possible and showing me how it's done! Sonja Jefferson was my guide for the first few iterations of the book proposal and helped me to put down its roots. Liz Gooster helped me more than she knows in sticking to my guns and writing the book I wanted to write. Richard Cunningham was kind enough to sanity check my maths and understanding of management accounting. Mindy Gibbins-Klein was instrumental in transforming this book from an idea to an actual document. Where Mindy helped me to start getting words on the page, my phenomenal editor Robert Watson helped me to stop, and be happy with the ones that were there! But, of course, it's not just a book of words. Neil Coe has been a pleasure to work with on the cover and layout design. Simon Ellinas is the creator of the fabulous cartoons that kick off each chapter, and working with Lizzie Everard on the diagrams and editorial illustrations really clarified my thinking. Thank you all.

Then, a word for my clients and other people who've shaped the thinking that has become Watertight Marketing. Firstly, Mark Mason for believing in me at age 22 and trusting me to grow into a role that became the platform for the career I love. Chris Archer-Brown – for whom appointing a 28-year-old director of marketing must have been a gamble – I cannot thank you enough for giving me this game-changing opportunity. Richard Tremellen, for challenging me to put together an irrefutable defence of marketing spending in a report that was the kernel of this book. A massive thanks also goes to all the clients of Clear Thought Consulting, especially those who were good enough to let me case study their companies: Peter Gradwell, Richard and Sarah Morfoot, Vince Wilton, Patrick Nash and Dave James. And, to those people who said yes when I asked to feature their businesses: Sonja Jefferson, Duane Jackson, John Watton, Chris Budd, Nick Ellis and David Gilroy. Professionally, and indeed personally, I couldn't possibly leave out Cheryl Crichton – a friend and colleague who has never let me down.

I'd also like to take this opportunity to thank one more person. My father. Dad – you will probably never know how grateful I am for the values, love and confidence you gave me. Perhaps it is fitting that you're at the bottom on this list, because you are the foundation on which all my successes have been built.

Thank you.

Academic Theories: Having worked in marketing for nearly two decades and undertaken various professional qualifications, I have encountered hundreds of marketing and management theories, concepts and models. I have made every attempt to highlight these throughout the text with the brain icon. More detail is provided on these at the end of the book with references to text books in which these theories are more deeply explored. The key six-step model on which the Watertight Marketing framework is based is an adapted version of Dr Philip Kotler's model of rational decision-making and it is duly acknowledged as such.

Copyright and Trademarks: So as not to interrupt the flow of the book for the reader copyright and trademark symbols have not been used within the body text. In addition to the businesses featured in case studies, the ownership of copyright, intellectual property and trademarks of the following companies and brands (listed alphabetically) are acknowledged: AdWords, Apple, Capsule, Facebook, Get Satisfaction, GoCompare, Google, Instagram, iPhone, Klout, LinkedIn, Mac, MailChimp, Microsoft, Orange, PeerIndex, Pinterest, Quora, RightNow, Road Runner, Salesforce.com, Sony Bravia, SugarCRM, Trollbeads, Twitter, Vimeo, Wile E. Coyote, YouTube.

Introduction

You work hard. So, let's make sure that you're getting the very best from every ounce of effort that you, and every member of your team, put into making your business a success. The best way to do this is to make sure that your business isn't leaking profit. However tight you think you have it, I've yet to encounter a business that couldn't step it up – by simply plugging the profit leaks.

Part One doesn't make for easy reading. It maps out leaks in your sales and marketing set-up that squander your precious funds and time. Taking a look at how real people really buy things, I expose the Thirteen Touchpoint Leaks, and turn the usual way of tackling them on its head for faster payback. Then you'll be introduced to the Four Foundation Leaks. These relate to marketing attitude and a company's internal workings. By the end of this section you'll have identified your major profit leaks from amongst these seventeen.

Part Two gets you to look at a purchasing decision from the buyer's perspective, mapping the way that real people really buy things onto the Watertight Marketing framework. It's an operational model that's easy to follow and means your marketing *will* deliver long-term sales results. You'll know what you need to say, how to say it, when, and to whom.

Just because you can draw a neat funnel, does not mean that there is one.

Part Three takes the concepts above and shows you how to apply them in practice. It works through fixing the Touchpoint Leaks with case studies and a fully worked example. It will equip any small business with what they need to plug the gaps they find. It challenges the picture that a classic sales funnel visual paints in your mind. Just because you can draw a neat funnel, does not mean that there is one. In reality, the buying decision, and the marketing and sales process a business has in place to support it, is much more irregular.

Every time you see, or refer to, a sales funnel or sales pipeline, I want you to re-imagine it as:

- **Your Taps:** Ways of generating interest in your offer.

- **Your Funnels:** The tools and techniques you use to channel that interest and move people through to trying you out.

- **Your Bucket:** Those things that come together to keep your customers your customers.

And, although it can seem tempting to put your energy into running those Taps as hard as you can, to really improve your profits, you'll be asked to start at the bottom and work up. If you keep this picture in mind, you'll quickly see why this is so critical. After all, there's no point running Taps if you can't Funnel the water. And, there's no point Funneling water to a Bucket that has a hole in it.

Part Four is about making this happen in your business. It closes off those Foundation Leaks, by showing you how to plan and pay for a Watertight Marketing operation, and then measure your success. What's more, your plan will be built to respond to ever-changing market conditions. You'll then be challenged to make marketing a good habit for the rest of your business life.

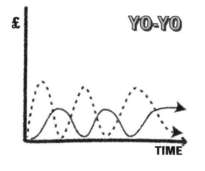

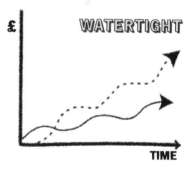

——————— MARKETING ACTIVITY

• • • • • • • • SALES RESULTS

Getting Watertight Marketing in place means that you can step off the exhausting roller coaster of being up one minute and down the next: selling then delivering, then selling then delivering, then selling then delivering – never quite reaching those sustainable, predictable and growing sales results that your small business needs to become a bigger business.

And, when that happens... who knows, someone might just come knocking with a big fat cheque with your name on it.

Your Watertight Marketing Workbook

Build your own plan as you go through the book by downloading your free Watertight Marketing Workbook. To get the most from this, have it it printed out with pen in hand as you go through the book.

Whenever you see this symbol you'll find the accompanying exercise in your workbook to complete.

Get your copy from **watertightmarketing.com**

And, then some lovely extras. You'll also see the following throughout:

A practical tip that you can get on with immediately.

An academic theory is being used and there's further reading detailed in the Brain Food section that you might find useful.

So, do you want to step up your business?

PART ONE

As a child I enjoyed watching the Road Runner cartoons; it was hilarious to watch Wile E Coyote go crashing down a ravine through a great big hole disguised as part of the road. It's not so funny to watch a potential customer crash out of their decision to buy from you because you've left a gap in the path. But, that is exactly what happens every day, to businesses large and small. Somewhere along the way there's a leap too far, and your potential new customer crosses you off their list.

YOU ARE LEAKING PROFIT

A buying decision is made in steps. How many steps is largely related to its importance. The less important the purchase, the fewer thought processes involved. Something like grabbing a coffee at a train station, or buying paperclips for the office, is pretty simple. The more important the decision, the more elongated it becomes. Like an annual family holiday, or a new software system for your company. It's a 'considered purchase'. And the more considered the purchase your buyers are making, the more relevant Watertight Marketing becomes.

The thought processes that a buyer goes through are the key to how you structure your marketing. You're not going to change human psychology. You can't shortcut their thinking. And, you shouldn't try. You absolutely should understand what these thought processes are, and why someone might count your business out when moving from one step to the next, which is addressed in Part Two. But before that, let's see where your business is currently leaking profit. By the end of this section you'll know which of the Thirteen Touchpoint Leaks affects your business. You'll also be able to identify whether your own attitude to marketing is leaving you victim to one or more of the Four Foundation Leaks.

> *You're not going to change human psychology. You can't shortcut their thinking. And, you shouldn't try.*

Their thinking = your marketing

When people are buying something that's important, expensive, or risky, they don't generally do it on a whim. They go through a few stages weighing up options and looking at alternatives. You will never find a magic formula that shortcuts the psychology. Every step on this journey is one where they could lose interest. By plugging gaps between stages, you will generate and retain more profitable customers.

A considered purchase

You'll see this process mapped out in various different ways in sales and marketing books going back decades. No one model fits every business, nor indeed every product, but the core principle remains that people don't go from blissful ignorance to paying customer in one great leap. They go through a series of thought processes along the way.

The more important or risky that decision, the more this seems to apply. At one end of the spectrum there are buying decisions made in a heartbeat. These are either impulse buys driven entirely by emotion or by logic, but rarely both. Those 'I just had to have it' moments, like a bunch of flowers or a chocolate bar. Or, something totally functional, like a pack of envelopes for the stationery cupboard. These kinds of decisions are made quickly and without reference to other people. If you were to ask buyers how they chose their goods in these cases, they probably couldn't break it down. There's a great deal of science and marketing expertise that goes into triggering an impulse purchase, but this book looks at the other end of the spectrum: the considered purchase.

In a considered purchase both emotional *and* rational appeals need to be met. This is because the buying decision tends to be more important, for one of the following reasons:

- **Expense:** there is a high financial outlay involved or an ongoing commitment.

- **Other people:** the purchase affects more than one person.

- **Status:** a person's sense of identity or reputation is affected by the purchase.

When these elements come together, the buyer has a lot to lose if they get their decision wrong. They are taking a risk. The job of your marketing is to reduce that risk.

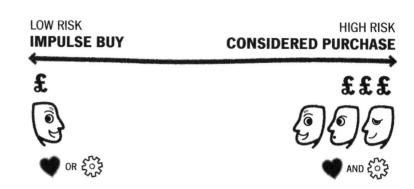

The further to the right a buyer would place their decision to buy what you're selling on this continuum, the more complex their thought processes are going to be.

 Run some research with your potential buyers or existing customers that asks them to place their buying decision on this continuum.

. . . .

 In your workbook

- How considered is your purchase?

. . . .

Most often you'll see this process depicted as a sales funnel. This is to represent a decreasing number of people moving from one step to the next, because people can cross you off their list at any of these stages. A sales funnel is usually labelled with internally-driven criteria, for example: Audience, Respondents, Leads, Qualified Leads, Proposals, Sales, and Renewals. Whilst this might serve a useful internal purpose, it doesn't help you to plan your marketing. It's a matter of cause and effect. The labels above are the effect, the thoughts of your buyers are the cause.

And, if you understand the cause, you will have more control over the effect. This means that you need to map *their* thinking, not *your* reporting systems.

> *If you understand the cause, you will have more control over the effect.*

The model that I've found most useful for getting a deeper understanding of the thought processes involved is a six-step one adapted from one originated by Dr Philip Kotler. It's useful for both business-to-business and personal buying decisions, and it goes like this:

A person has some sort of need...

1. **Awareness:** They notice that you offer something that could help.

2. **Interest:** They decide to find out a little bit more.

3. **Evaluation:** They see if you look credible.

4. **Trial:** They find out what it would be like to buy from you.

5. **Adoption:** They become a customer.

6. **Loyalty:** They keep buying, buy more, and/or tell others about you.

The reporting metrics mentioned earlier are the result of a person moving from one thought to the next. You should substitute these internally-driven labels with ones that indicate the stage of the purchasing decision in terms of *their* thinking. This will enable you to understand your buyers better.

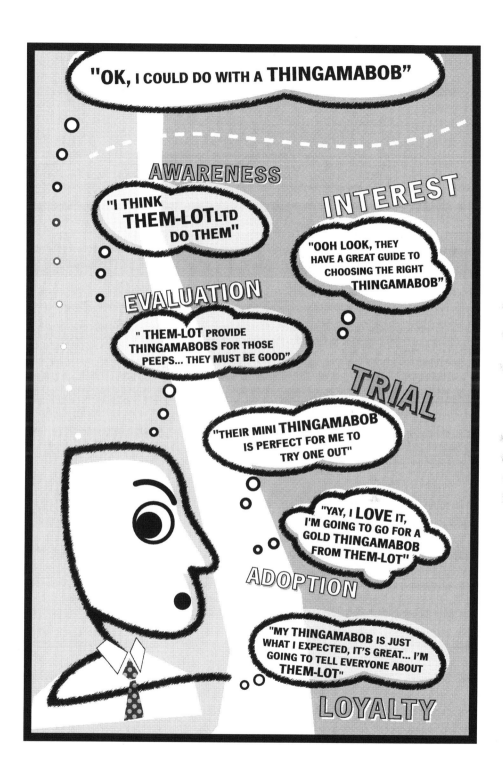

You might report the effect	Their thought processes are the cause
Audience	Awareness
Respondents	Interest
Leads or Qualified Leads	Evaluation
Proposals	Trial
Sales	Adoption
Renewals	Loyalty

It can be helpful to overlay their thinking on your sales funnel. Then ask yourself: have I laid a clear path to my door? Different marketing tools and techniques are more effective at different stages. But, for each step there is a core purpose or task for your marketing to address. If you put together an integrated set of tools and materials that meet these tasks, more people will make it all the way through to Loyalty. And, you'll make more money.

A marketing task for each step

Many businesses see the task of marketing as generating leads for salespeople to follow-up. It's a short-sighted view that is costing small businesses millions. Marketing is the *whole process* of taking your goods or services to market. It's made up of many different disciplines, each with their own skills and expertise. But, at its core, marketing has six tasks. One for each step in a buyer's thought process.

> *It's a short-sighted view that is costing small businesses millions.*

Step 1: generating **AWARENESS**
This is what most people think marketing is all about. It's getting your name known. For this you need to **be there.** Find out where your buyers hang out, in person or online, and make sure your business is represented.

Step 2: stimulating **INTEREST**
Let's imagine that someone knows of your company, and they've started to think about buying something along the lines of what you sell. You need to draw them in with something of Interest. For this you need to **be relevant.** Find out the questions they're asking themselves at this moment. Answer them.

Step 3: surviving **EVALUATION**
Once you've gained their Interest, people will start weighing up whether you meet their buying criteria. They'll be looking for evidence that you can deliver what you say you can. Here, you need to **be proven.** For every promise you make, you need to provide proof.

Step 4: enabling **TRIAL**
If you've survived scrutiny to the extent that your potential buyer believes that your company is a real contender for their business, the next step is for them to establish a sense of what it would be like if they bought from you. For this, you need to **be helpful.** Facilitate some way of your buyer experiencing being your customer before

they become one. Don't tell them; *show* them just how much you'd resolve their problem or satisfy their need.

Step 5: securing **ADOPTION**
It's essential to recognise that people will often go with their gut at this critical hurdle. As such, you need to **be friendly** to ensure that they feel comfortable working with you. This can often be by virtue of your company being known by someone else in their circle. This means that you need to be friendly to everyone who could have their ear. This works like Commercial Karma.

Step 6: encouraging **LOYALTY**
Here you need to ensure that a customer is in fact a customer in their own mind, rather than just on your books. And, you need to make sure that they remember why they chose you in the first place. To do this you need to **be consistent**. This is a big one. You'll need to be consistent to the expectations you set through the sales process. You'll need to be consistent with the style of interaction that's been established. And, you'll need to remain consistent in talking to, and valueing, your customers. Effectively, you need to be consistently doing all of the above. All of the time.

Their step...	The marketing task...
AWARENESS	Be There
INTEREST	Be Relevant
EVALUATION	Be Proven
TRIAL	Be Helpful
ADOPTION	Be Friendly
LOYALTY	Be Consistent

Across the six steps you'd imagine that there are five potential leaks, as people don't make the leap from one to the other. That's certainly a good place to start. But, digging a little deeper exposes Thirteen Touchpoint Leaks. Each one is a gap through which you could lose potential paying customers for your business. And, assuming you have a sound business model – more customers means more profit.

> *Assuming you have a sound business model – more customers means more profit.*

Identify your leaks

I want you turn your thinking about your sales funnel on its head. I want you, for the moment, to stop thinking about how to pour more into the top and look instead from the bottom up. This way, when you do come to spend time, money and energy telling the world about what you do, you'll get more back. In fact, by addressing the leaks from the bottom up you won't need to pour as much in the top to get the same, or better, results.

The Thirteen Touchpoint Leaks

Leak #1 – Forgotten customers

Look first to the people who've been on your books for a while. It's easy to think that once you've got them the hard work is over. Unfortunately, your business just isn't the most important thing on their list, so it's easy for them to forget about you. If you have customers paying an annual fee for something, but when the invoice comes around they've forgotten who you are and why they bought from you in the first place, you have a potential leak. And, that's quite apart from telling them about anything else you might have on offer.

The risk of simply forgetting stuff is borne out time after time in educational studies. In the UK, there's lots of talk of re-jigging the school year to reduce the traditional 6-week summer holiday, because the first half of the autumn term is spent re-learning the stuff they studied just before the holiday. And, that's fresh young minds... just imagine how quickly busy business people move on to the next important thing. Forgetting your customers is a surefire way of losing their Loyalty.

Leak #2 – Poor on-boarding

Now, look to those people who've just signed-up. For a buyer, there's a critical period between placing an order and considering themselves a loyal customer. It's the period in which a customer is sussing out whether a company is living up to the expectations they had. Exactly how long this period is will depend on what your company offers. For an online retail business, it might be until your product has been received and tried out for the first time. For a consultancy business, it might be after your first workshop in a longer consulting exercise. Whatever your business model, there will be an interval between when someone places an order, and when they really consider themselves a loyal customer of yours.

Between these two moments you could lose a person on whom you've spent a great deal of time, money and energy. In that time, these people may appear on your books as a paying customer. But, psychologically, they're not. And, it is critical to real Adoption that your customers are customers in their own minds, not just on your systems. To address this you need a systemic approach to customer on-boarding.

Leak #3 – No emotional connection

Have you ever lost a deal only to find that it went instead to someone that the buyer plays golf with? Okay, so perhaps we've not all experienced that exact scenario, but I'm sure most businesses can empathise with the sense that there are times when it's not the best person who wins, it's the one the buyer likes most. Having an emotional connection can be all important in getting people over that final hurdle. You can have ticked all their logical boxes, but if it doesn't feel right, often there's no deal. To stem this leak you need to be the kind of people that buyers want to deal with. Securing Adoption means securing an emotional connection.

> *You can have ticked all their logical boxes, but if it doesn't feel right, often there's no deal.*

Part Two provides the strategic backdrop to these issues. The really critical piece on balancing your emotional and logical messaging is covered specifically in chapter three. Chapter six looks at these three leaks in detail, with straightforward guidance for addressing each.

Leak #4 – No gateway

Your on-boarding might be brilliant, but what about people who don't get that far? If you don't give people a sense of what it's like to work with you, or use your stuff, before they part with a large sum of money, you're going to lose a few potential customers. It's like trying on clothes – there's no other way of knowing if they fit and suit you. In a knowledge-based business, or a product or service that's less tangible, you'll need to work harder. But the principle is the same. You need to find a way of allowing people some sort of Trial. This may be an unpaid taster session or event, or you could design a Gateway Product that acts as a stepping stone between thinking about buying from you and actually buying from you.

Leak #5 – No critical approval

Then there's the outside world. Considered buying decisions aren't made in a vacuum. Before people go to the trouble of undertaking a Trial, they'll often consult others. In a family, people will ask, and want the tacit or explicit approval of, their partners and children. In a peer group, people will turn to their friends (virtual or actual). In a business, people don't just consult but will often need to get formal approval from colleagues or their boss. Whenever your potential buyer seeks the opinion of a third party, you risk losing the sale. At this stage in the process, other people can't just influence the decision; they can often veto it altogether.

Leak #6 – No proof

Assuming that you have someone's attention, usually with an emotional message, their logical brain will start to kick in. This is when they're weighing you up, usually against two things: the promises you've made and their specific list of buying criteria. This is a process of Evaluation, and it's broadly logical.

Emotion is important, but, this doesn't mean that you can simply woo a person right through to signing on the bottom line.

Emotion is important, but, this doesn't mean that you can simply woo a person right through to signing on the bottom line. The more expensive or important the purchase, the more likely they are to ask questions and look for logical validation for their decision. If you avoid giving answers, you'll look slippery and untrustworthy. It's like asking a salesperson the price, and they reply that the colour really suits you... it feels all wrong. And, in most cases it will lose you the sale. What you need here are answers and evidence.

Again, chapter three is critical in getting that logic and emotion in the right order. Chapter five is all about a strategic approach to third parties. Specific fixes for these three leaks are provided in chapter seven.

Leak #7 – Information overload

How many marketing messages do you think you're exposed to every day? If you're living in a capitalist economy it's been estimated to be 3000! And, this is on top of the other things you have on your mind, like your to-do list, getting the kids' gym kit ready, calling your Dad. You know, the things that really matter.

Your buyers have busy lives. If you make it hard, or time-consuming, for them to find out about you, they're going to go elsewhere. That's not to say that over the course of a considered purchase they won't give the decision quite a lot of time; they just don't do it all at once. They're far more likely to make the decision over a period of time, with increasing levels of attention (and time taken) as they move closer to the purchase. You need to break it down and draw them in, providing them information in the right quantity for them to digest in increasing chunks as they choose to give it more time. If you present all the information all at once, you're very likely to put people off. You won't stimulate their Interest. It's just too much information, too soon. Instead you need effective invitation information. That is information that's useful, entertaining or thought-provoking, and can be digested alongside a cup of tea.

> *If you present all the information all at once, you're very likely to put people off.*

Leak #8 – Not representing your business for _how_ they're looking

Different people like different types of information. Furthermore, different people may respond to the same information better when it's presented in another way. For example, video is increasingly popular for younger buyers, whilst a Chief Executive will probably still have a PA to print something out to read on the train. And, of course – not everyone is online. Although a small and decreasing percentage, there are people who either don't have, or don't like to use, the Internet. It's certainly the case that many people look online, then print off something they may want to read whilst sitting on the sofa. So, if you're pursuing an entirely digital approach, you are actively choosing not to talk to some people. You're actively limiting the possible levels of Awareness by not accessing some people.

Leak #9 – Not represented _where_ they're looking

So, assuming that you have excellent information, in the right format, you now need to get it in front of the right people. If you're not in the right place, people just won't know you're there.

Many people assume that search engines are a natural starting point for buying journeys. But, in recent years many purchases started with an enquiry on YouTube, Twitter or Facebook. Think about it. There are so many ways for people to start researching a purchase these days, they could:

- Ask a friend.

- Ask their 'friends' on Facebook.

- Ask their 'followers' on Twitter.

- Ask their 'connections' on LinkedIn.

- See a 'pin' on Pinterest.

- Ask a question on Quora.

- Do a search using a search engine.

- Do a search using a social media site.

- Happen across an article whilst reading about something else.

- Spot an ad that catches their eye on the bus to work.

- Hear an ad on the radio when washing up.

- Have a look on a directory website or book (Yellow Pages still works for manual trades for example).

- And so many more ways... every day.

If you're not where they are looking, you've missed them. There will be no chance of securing their Awareness.

Leak #10 – Not there _when_ they're looking

To gain a person's Awareness, your company will need to come to mind, and to hand (or eye, or ear), at the moment that a potential buyer is in the market for what you're selling. You might run a 9am-5pm operation, but they might do their research on the sofa in the evening. People in senior positions will often be found working 50+ hours a week, so it's not unusual for them to think about buying decisions in the evening, at the weekend, or on that early train or flight to a meeting. And, if your potential buyers span different time zones, you might well be asleep when they have important questions to ask.

Leak #11 – Not known by _who_ they ask

The beginning of many buying decisions will start with the buyer asking around. In the early stages of researching a purchase, people will cast the net quite wide reducing down to key people as they draw closer to their decision. So, it's not just those people affected by the decision, like in Leak #5, it's a much larger pool. In a socially-

From official review sites, to posting a question on Twitter, your buyers can, and will, ask other people for their opinion.

networked world, the sheer quantity of third party opinions is mind boggling. From official review sites, to posting a question on Twitter, your buyers can, and will, ask other people for their opinion. Knowing who your buyers are likely to turn to when doing their initial research, and finding ways to make sure that your company is in their minds, stops these kinds of missed opportunities, and leaked profits. What this means in practice is that you need to consider the impact of every encounter with your business, directly or indirectly. A person who may seem insignificant on paper may in fact have the ear of your next big customer. Nobody is nobody.

Leak #12 – Not known for <u>what</u> you do

Probably the most galling of all the leaks, is when someone who knows about your company, or even an existing customer, goes to a competitor for something you offer. And, when you ask them why they tell you that they didn't know you provided that. One of my clients offers IT services to small businesses. Effectively, they act as a virtual IT department doing the full range of IT support. They also sell a few packaged products, like hosted email. Just as we started working together, they had a request to terminate a hosted email product because the client in question was moving all of their services to another company offering the full service IT support they now wanted. When asked why they hadn't considered my client for this, they said that they just didn't know that was on offer. If a customer, potential customer, or those all-important influencers have your company incorrectly filed in their minds, then you have a leak in your profits. This is when you have Awareness, but for the wrong thing.

If a customer, potential customer, or those all-important influencers have your company incorrectly filed in their minds, then you have a leak in your profits.

Leak #13 – No emotional impact

Last on the list, but by no means least in importance, is getting your emotional messaging right up front. We've talked about having the right fit to secure the sale, and having the right evidenced arguments when the logical brain kicks in. However, if you've not grabbed someone's attention in the first place, none of this matters.

 Human beings are built to respond to particular stimuli. From very early in life we respond to emotional prompts instinctively – things like smiles or danger. It's only later that we learn to reason, and start responding to logical arguments. This is why emotional stimuli are almost always better at grabbing a person's attention, and generating initial Awareness.

It's only later that we learn to reason, and start responding to logical arguments.

You need to capture someone emotionally before giving them the logical arguments. I like to tell people that you can't logic someone into love – and the first step in a buying decision is pretty similar. If you logic people too soon, you'll usually lose the sale.

Part Two provides the holistic view of where these issues sit in a Watertight Marketing framework. Specific guidance on getting something appropriate in place to stem each of these remaining seven leaks is the focus of chapter eight.

These Thirteen Touchpoint Leaks are the ones that relate to the process you have in place to support the buying decision. But, that's not the only way in which you could be leaking profit in your marketing operation. So far we've only looked at potential leaks that stem from how you interact with the outside world. However, your internal behaviour, and attitude to marketing, can in itself be leaky.

....

 In your workbook

- Touchpoint Leak Traffic Light

....

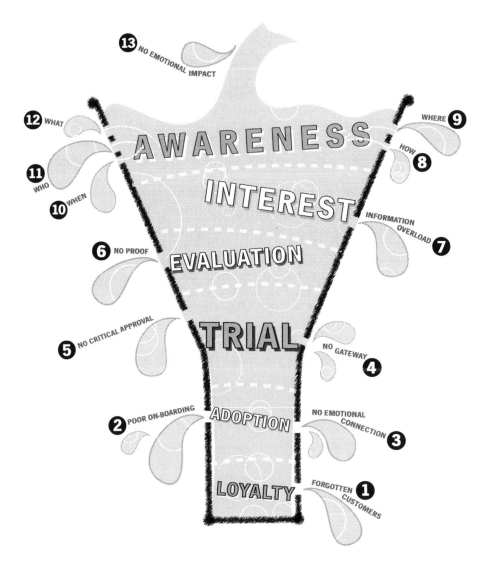

The Four Foundation Leaks

Many of the leaks above are symptomatic of underlying, foundational issues. A pattern of peaks and troughs will often emerge. A big bit of business comes in, and it's all hands to the pumps. People get their heads down to deliver the paying piece of work. Whilst they're doing so there's little time and energy available for telling people about your business in order to secure the next deal, or the one after that. Let's imagine that your business has been hard at it delivering a 12-week project for a demanding client. In that time none of your team has been to any networking events, or updated your website, or gained any press coverage, or done anything to maintain your presence in the marketplace. You've effectively turned the Taps off. At the end of the twelve weeks, you have a happy client and an empty Bucket. Businesses that experience this are likely to be suffering one of these Four Foundation Leaks.

Leak #14 – The wrong kind of work

The most damaging effect I've seen with this roller coaster approach to marketing is that businesses often end up accepting work that's not ideal. Because they've let the Taps run dry they feel forced to accept paying work of any kind, even if it's not the most profitable or enjoyable. There's a double dip in this one. Taking work that's not quite the right fit, which then takes your full focus for a period of time, means that you're less able to tell people about the work you really want to be doing. Which, in turn, means you end up in a downward spiral of becoming known for stuff you don't really want to do – moving further away from what you do want to do. Most often this is about clarity of purpose and the willpower of the business owner. Key chapters for this are chapter six and eleven.

> *Because they've let the Taps run dry they feel forced to accept paying work of any kind, even if it's not the most profitable or enjoyable.*

Leak #15 – Unused marketing muscles

Marketing skills, like any others, are at their sharpest when regularly exercised. If your business is only picking them up sporadically, like when the pipeline looks dry, you're necessarily lacking some muscle tone. Even if you're working with third party experts, there's the time to find them and brief them that just makes the on/off approach less effective. What's more, with digital marketing techniques in particular, the pace of change is rapid – dipping in and out will often mean constantly playing catch up. Getting marketing fit is such an important topic, it's covered throughout, and specifically addressed in chapter eleven.

Leak #16 – No familiarity to work from

If you've gone quiet for a while, it's likely that people will be less familiar with you. Let's imagine that you met someone at a networking event, but only get around to calling them weeks later – you'll forgive them for not immediately recalling you or your company. What's typical for a company in this rhythm is to rely on cold sales techniques to re-fill the pipeline. The paying work goes quiet, so energy is diverted to calling through the database to drum up some business. And, because you've gone quiet for a while, much of the call is taken up explaining who you are and what you do. How much better it would be to pick up the phone to someone who says "From XYZ Ltd? Oh, yes I read a case study of yours in Tractors Weekly just yesterday. Looks like you're doing some great stuff", rather than "Sorry, who are you again?" Maintaining market Awareness is what you're after – which is covered in chapter five specifically. It's about having a 'little and often' approach, which exactly what the Baseline Budget in chapter nine delivers.

"Sorry, who are you again?"

Leak #17 – Expensive exhaustion

This yo-yo cycle can be exhausting. Being up one minute and down the next is a rough ride on your emotions, and that of your team. And, if you've also taken on a few of those not-so-perfect projects, then it's likely that your staff aren't best pleased. If you employ someone on the basis that they'll be doing X, which they love, but they end up doing Y, which they don't, you have a recipe for high employee turnover. And, we all know how disruptive and expensive finding new employees can be. What's more, that person is then out there telling the world that your business isn't quite what it says it is. They then potentially become that critical third party who puts a buyer off as described in Leak #5. If exhaustion is an issue, you're going to need to find something that really inspires you to dig deep on those energy reserves to make the step up you want for your business. Chapters eight and eleven are particularly pertinent to this.

Your business won't have all of these seventeen leaks. If you're in business, and paying the bills, you're clearly doing a lot right. But, I'm willing to bet if you were setting each to Red, Amber and Green, one or two would be flashing red. And, even those that aren't high on your list to address, a little tweak here and there could have a healthy effect on your bottom line.

In your workbook

- Foundation Leak Traffic Light

Sales funnels don't exist

So far we've looked at a fairly typical sales funnel. But, sales funnels are misleading. If you pour water into the top of a funnel, every drop will come out at the bottom. If only that were true in translation to your profit and loss account. In reality, interest in your business comes from many and varied sources, and a person's path to your door is often more of a zigzag than a straight line. And, unfortunately, not everyone who becomes a customer stays a customer. It's much more powerful to visualise your marketing operation as being made up of three parts – your Bucket, your Funnels, and your Taps.

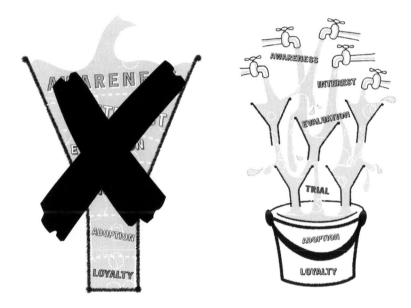

It's only when you have these three things in place, and lined up, that it's possible to secure ongoing, profitable, sales for your business.

And, that's what Watertight Marketing is all about.

SUMMARY OF PART ONE

The more important the decision the longer someone will think about it. In this time they will move through a series of interlinked thoughts until they have reassured themselves that they are making the right choice. This extended thought process can be helpfully broken down into six steps, and for each step there is a particular task for your marketing to perform. If your company doesn't stay on a person's list of potential organisations to buy from as they move from one stage in the process to the next, you've lost a sale. There are thirteen key points at which you're in touch with that person – each representing a potential leak in your new business pipeline.

Their step	Your task	Touchpoint Leaks
AWARENESS	Be There	#13 No emotional impact
		#12 What
		#11 Who
		#10 When
		#9 Where
		#8 How
INTEREST	Be Relevant	#7 Information overload
EVALUATION	Be Proven	#6 No proof
TRIAL	Be Helpful	#5 No critical approval
		#4 No gateway
ADOPTION	Be Friendly	#3 No emotional connection
		#2 Poor on-boarding
LOYALTY	Be Consistent	#1 Forgotten customers

Seeing this process not as the linear one that's often depicted, but instead as made up of a Bucket, Funnels and Taps, quickly reveals why addressing these issues one by one and from the bottom up will definitely improve your sales results. However, this will only be maintained in the long term if you also address the Four Foundation Leaks to make marketing part of the fibre of your business.

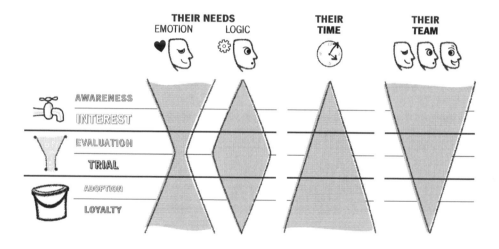

THEIR NEEDS

EMOTION   LOGIC

THEIR TIME

THEIR TEAM

AWARENESS

INTEREST

EVALUATION

TRIAL

ADOPTION

LOYALTY

Understanding how real people really buy things is central to getting your business onto an upward curve. Your products and services can be the most innovative, effective, beautiful or useful things on the planet and still not achieve great sales results. It's only when other people believe this that you're onto a winner.

First there's the psychology of it all. For this you need to master The Logic Sandwich. There's an interplay between the left and right sides of the brain. To win that new customer, you'll need to appeal to both. You'll need emotion to catch their attention, logic to address their specific requirements, and emotion to cement the relationship. Address these needs in the wrong order and you will lose the sale. This is about your message. It's about knowing what to say, and when.

As with so many things, timing is crucial. Again, I want you to turn the normal way of approaching this on its head. Don't think about how long you need to explain your offer, think about how you can explain your offer in the amount of time your buyer is willing to give you. Responding to the pace your buyer sets means more sales and longer-lasting relationships. This is about more than getting your timing right. It's about earning the right to take up a person's time.

And then, there's the outside world. Buying decisions aren't made in a vacuum. I want you to think about who is on your buyer's team. That is, whose opinion matters to them as they are making their decision. When drawing up a long list of companies they might buy from, people may cast the net quite wide. This is becoming wider by the minute with social media taking root. But, as they get nearer to parting with their hard-earned money, they will tend to turn to a decreasing number of select people. You need those people to say the right things about you at the right time. This is about your extended audience. It's about knowing who to talk to, at what point in the process.

> *I want you to think about who is on their team.*

Their needs = your messages

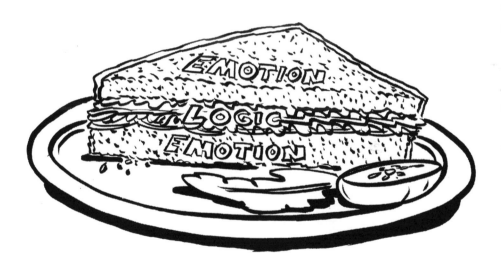

To successfully take people through a whole buying decision, you need to find the right balance between satisfying their emotional and logical needs. The human brain has two halves: the left side of the brain is rational, considered and thoughtful, the right is creative, intuitive and spontaneous. To really get someone on board, you need to appeal to both sides of their nature. In short, you need messages that tick their emotional and logical boxes.

The Logic Sandwich

Whatever you're selling and whomever you're selling it to, in the vast majority of cases you are selling to a person: a human being. Even in a business-to-business context where a whole industry exists to ensure robust logical decision making, there are still real people making the final choices. Computerised bidding systems and blind auctions are still the exception. And, real people are primarily driven by their emotions. Even when what they articulate is a logical motivation for a purchase, there will be an emotional driver behind that. For example, a manager may logically want to increase productivity in the workplace. This makes great business sense, but might really be because he'd be less stressed if he could go home feeling that he's done a good job, or in time to read his children a bedtime story. There are always two sides to a decision, and you need to satisfy both.

This is about what to say, and, crucially, when to say it. You need to satisfy the different types of need in a particular order: start with emotion, move on to logic, and then return to emotion. It's what I've taken to calling The Logic Sandwich.

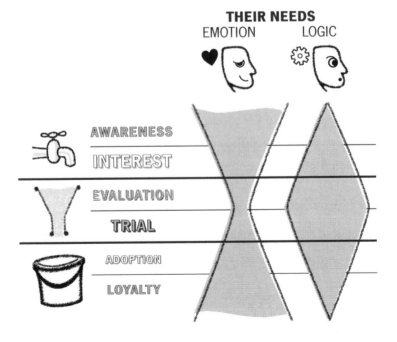

Marketers will often talk about finding your killer message or 'unique selling point'. This supposes that there's one magic message that will get people to buy your stuff. In reality, there are a series of connected messages that differ according to the thought process a person is going through at the time and in relation to a given decision.

Messaging for momentum

A buying decision is a journey. And, you need to keep people moving. The emotional and logical content of what you say is at the core of maintaining this momentum.

It can be helpful to think about a family choosing a new home. They may be prompted into action by the arrival of a new child. They start to see their home as cramped and imagine it will be uncomfortable for a larger family. In the case of a first child, where they're living may not be the kind of place they want to raise children. There's a problem to solve. They'll draw up a list of the things they need from a new family home: number of rooms, parking, proximity to good schools, garden space, etc. They'll also be mindful of logical constraints, like their budget, how much renovation they could take on, and driving distance from their place of work. Then, they'll start the search. The logical criteria will rule things in or out. But, very often the place a family ends up buying is the one that they 'had a good feeling about'. Indeed, compromises are often made on the wish list, or budgets stretched to breaking point, for somewhere that feels like home. In this scenario, they were jolted into action by a problem and the negative emotion that goes with that, they logically reassured themselves of their choices

> *Indeed, compromises are often made on the wish list, or budgets stretched to breaking point, for somewhere that feels like home.*

against a list of specific criteria, but the final decision was very much driven by the heart and the positive picture of a comfortable family life. And, this, to a greater or lesser extent, is the journey you're trying to replicate for people who buy from you.

Their step	Your task	Your message	Emotion	Logic
AWARENESS	Be There	Do you feel like this?	High	Low
INTEREST	Be Relevant	This is what you could do about it	Medium	Medium
EVALUATION	Be Proven	See how it's worked for others	Low	High
TRIAL	Be Helpful	This is what you need to make it happen	Low	High
ADOPTION	Be Friendly	Imagine how great it would be	Medium	Medium
LOYALTY	Be Consistent	Is everything still great?	High	Low

What this example also demonstrates, is that of the two sorts of appeal, emotion is the most important because it tops and tails the process.

However, there's more than one type of emotional appeal. And, you need to choose the right one, at the right time. There are: positive emotions, like joy or humour, and negative emotions like fear and pain. Any of these emotional appeals can make an excellent basis for your messaging. If you take a moment next time you're watching television to consider the ads, you'll almost certainly see each of these being used. But, to make most effective use of your budget, you'll need to balance your use of each and consider where in the process you use them.

Negative emotions are the most effective for initiating action, because a person will naturally do something to move themselves away from the feelings. Because they initiate action they work well at the top of the process. Positive emotions are useful throughout, but are essential in the latter stages of a purchasing decision, or as the basis for your company's brand. This is because, they make people feel comfortable and reduce their sense of risk. This also builds Loyalty as they enjoy the positive feelings, and breeds inertia to change making it less likely that they'll move to a competitor.

You will often be vying for a person's attention amongst a clutter of other messages and priorities. An emotional response can cut through this because it's something that seems to *happen to* us, rather than something we *choose to* do. It's instinctive. This is why it's so important to generating Awareness and Interest where the aim here is to get someone to find out more about your offer. This means *doing* something. Hitting an emotional trigger means that people can't help but notice you. Hitting a negative trigger means they can't help but want to do something about it.

> *An emotional response can cut through this because it's something that seems to happen to us, rather than something we choose to do.*

This is why you'll hear marketers asking you to think about 'the point of pain' that your product or service addresses. By this they mean what problem does it solve? You're missing a trick here if the problem you focus on is inherently logical; you need to get to the emotion behind that. For example, storage solutions logically gives a person a place to put things. So, you might think that the problem you're solving is where to put things. But, the emotional need might be that seeing mess everywhere stresses them out. The negative emotion that a person will want to move away from is the stress. This is the emotional pain that they're really trying to relieve. Breaking this down into logical tasks (like buying some storage boxes) is just what they need to do to achieve that. Fear, another negative emotion that can also trigger action, is particularly powerful if you want people to recognise a need that they don't immediately think they have.

It's worth noting that you need to make sure that the fear or pain you depict is realistic. If you overstate your case, people will immediately discount it. In our storage example above, if you made the claim that the trip hazard of a messy house is a life threatening danger, the human brain would quickly dismiss this on the basis of probability. But, if you hooked into that daily feeling of being irritated or weighed down by clutter and mess everywhere you turn, you're more likely to get a response.

CASE STUDY: Ascentor

Information risk consultants, Ascentor, help organisations to ensure that their business information is appropriately secure. They found that many companies they talked to didn't see a need for their services because they had a technical solution in place, like encryption or firewalls. They needed to help people recognise that information security was not just an IT issue. To do this, Ascentor used a negative emotion: fear. They commissioned a poll, verifiable proof, that found over half of the UK workforce willing to compromise their employer, by way of its information, in retaliation for perceived mistreatment, like being passed over for promotion. The survey exposed frightening figures on employees having already stolen data or passed information to competitors. They used this to run an awareness campaign that helped people visualise this very real, and very human, risk factor. This was used to drive people to an event where Ascentor presented ways to resolve these issues, providing those all-important positive emotions.

Your message needs to be strong enough to make them want to change, but it mustn't make them feel demoralised or violated.

You need to take care when using negative appeals. People don't like the company of negative people. And, unless your business offers some sort of therapeutic service, delving too deep can backfire. So, whilst negative messages can be great for initiating action, nobody responds well to feeling like they are being emotionally manipulated. Your message needs to be strong enough to make them want to change, but it mustn't make them feel demoralised or violated. Whenever you use a negative trigger, you need to quickly provide the remedying positive feelings that people want to move towards so that people to seek comfort in your solution.

When to say what

Most companies have a lot of the right messages. It's the order they get wrong. This manifests in a number of ways I'm sure you'll recognise. They'll be trying to convince people to find out more with dazzling logic that goes unnoticed. They'll seem evasive by not switching to logic when their buyer has. Or, they'll spoil the moment by continuing to rationalise when people simply want to feel good about their decision.

Lost in logic

If you're too logical too soon, you will find people are actively put off, or simply don't notice you. Listing your facts and figures just doesn't tick that emotional box, and the sale is lost before the journey has even begun.

It's called 'features-based selling' and it assumes that your buyer will be able to look at the factual information on the features you're presenting and interpret what that will mean in their life. It's an assumption that rules out a vast proportion of the buying public, who are busy getting on with their lives and need an emotional trigger to prompt them into listening to what you have to say.

> *It's an assumption that rules out a vast proportion of the buying public, who are busy getting on with their lives.*

Technology companies are particularly poor at getting this the wrong way around. You can tell me until I'm blue in the face how much memory a computer has, but if I don't realise that this will mean my documents stop crashing whilst I'm working on them,

I just won't care. Ascentor, above, has exceptional credentials with consultants qualified in all sorts of industry standards and excellent processes for uncovering all areas of information risk in a business; but none of this is relevant if the potential buyer doesn't think they have a problem.

Emotion can appear evasive

It's only when you've triggered the emotional response that people become interested in the logical side of your offering. Once people feel that they have a problem and are excited that you may provide the solution, they will switch into a logical frame of mind where they seek to verify that.

Most of us were taught in high school to look for evidence to substantiate any bold claims.

At this point, they start to evaluate your offer against the promise you've made (of solving their problem). They're looking for proof. Without it, you're effectively asking people to trust you with no evidence. And, most of us were taught in high school to look for evidence to substantiate any bold claims. Check that you're doing this. Wherever you make a bold claim, is there a signpost directing the buyer to where they can find the evidence? For example, do you have a client testimonial or case study sitting alongside your product information?

Substantiating any claims is essential. If you can't do this, most people will cross you off their list. In the middle part of the process, your buyer will be looking at the practicalities. You'll need to equip them with everything they need to know to actually make the purchase. They'll be looking for things like:

- How much it costs

- What's included in the price

- How long it will take

- Whether it fits with their existing set-up.

What's really interesting about a buyer who's switched into logic, is that emotional appeals now become an irritation. Imagine...

- Q: Who else uses it? A: You won't regret buying it.

- Q: How much is this? A: It will change your life.

- Q: How long will it take to arrive? A: You will love it when it does.

- Q: What are the key measurements? A: You'll want to show it to everyone.

Now, these aren't great answers even if someone was in an emotional frame of mind, but if their brain is in a logical gear these sorts of answers seem evasive and unhelpful. It's exactly the sort of salesmanship that you'll hear people describe as 'slippery', or 'wouldn't answer a straight question'.

When potential buyers are looking for logical answers, you must provide them. Whether that's in person, in store, online, etc. This information is essential – but, at the right time. The middle part of the process is the time to list off those evidenced features.

Don't spoil the moment

Once you've ticked a person's logical boxes, you will find that they switch back into emotion. It's almost like a sigh of relief as they reach a decision that they're happy with. You need to recognise this switch, and validate it.

You need to find a way of ending the journey on a high. At the beginning you were pricking a pain point, however you're now giving them a sense of relief and excitement that their pain is about to go away. You need to make sure that your sales journey ends with your buyer picturing themselves better off as your customer. This is what people will want to move towards and it will keep them moving in the right direction.

This is where positive emotions, and human interaction, are extremely powerful. To get them through to a purchase you need to ensure that they can picture themselves enjoying the outcome. Simply having an enjoyable chat with them via social media can assist this. What's certain is that if you keep banging on about all the logical reasons to buy your stuff when someone has already mentally made that decision, you can spoil the moment.

The long-term benefits

Reduce perceived risk

In an important buying decision people are looking to mitigate risk. A person's instinct is critical to their perception of risk. So, what you'll find in a considered buying context, is that if all things are logically equal, a person will go with the company or product that *feels* right. In fact, people will often forego some of the logical aspects if the fit is good. This is particularly true in situations where they'll be working with your people. If everything looks brilliant on paper, but the people don't seem to gel, they may well go with the logically inferior proposition. You'll only achieve this feeling if you've ticked their emotional boxes. This is about earning a person's trust.

> *If all things are logically equal, a person will go with the company or product that feels right.*

Emotion also explains why people often choose a brand they know well. Just at the point that someone is going to sign on the dotted line, there's an emotional tug that asks 'are you sure?' – a well established brand, or a level of familiarity, can overcome this final hurdle. If your company is one that they've seen consistently represented, or they've come to know and like your people in social media, and they feel clear about what to expect from you, that trust is likely to be there – and the sale is yours.

Reduce price sensitivity

Trust also explains why people are willing to pay more for a brand they know well. A brand becomes a kind of shorthand. Over time the brand becomes associated with quality standards and a way of doing business. This means that people don't feel the need to scrutinise the offer as much as they would one from an unknown company. So, if it's a choice between something they already trust at a higher price, or something cheaper from a company they've never heard of, people are often willing to trade the time they'd need to put in to finding out about the latter for paying the higher price.

Improve business sustainability

An emotional bond is also a fantastically valuable asset in terms of the sustainability of your business. If people have an emotional connection with your company, they will forgive you mistakes. The Apple iPhone 4 antennae issue was a prime example of this. The new phone from the lifestyle technology brand was launched amidst a maelstrom of rumour about a flaw that affected its core functionality – that of making and receiving calls. After a period of silence, and then denial, they issued a cover to rectify the (alleged) issue. But, in this period sales didn't slow one bit. And, devotees were quick to jump to their defence. You don't have to be a multi-billion dollar company to develop this sort of trust from your customers. In fact, smaller businesses can often build more authentic connections with their buyers because there are fewer of them. Social media has put the tools to do this in the hands of any business at negligible cost.

> *If people have an emotional connection with your company, they will forgive you mistakes.*

CASE STUDY: Fable Trading

When Fable Trading, the UK distributors of premium jewellery brand, Trollbeads, ran their first UK fan convention, they were a victim of their own success. Having never run a customer event before, they were overwhelmed by the volume of fans wanting to attend to meet jewellery designers, see beads being made, and receive a special gift. As a result, there were simply too many attendees for the venue they had chosen, and a number of people were disappointed by long queues and poor visibility. The company's Facebook page and Twitter feed was soon busy with customers expressing their feelings. Overnight, and without prompting from the company, a fan set up an area on the Facebook page for other fans to leave feedback and suggestions for getting it right next time. When the company then posted a blog responding to feedback, they were able to thank customers for their excellent suggestions and make sure people knew they were being heard.

In your workbook

- Emotional appeals

- Logical appeals

- Map your messages

Key points

- Start with emotion, go onto logic, then back to emotion.

- Negative emotions are best at kicking off a buying journey.

- Positive emotions are important for maintaining momentum.

- Logic alone will rarely stop someone in their tracks or get an instinctive response.

- Emotional answers to logical questions seem slippery.

- Making an emotional connection reduces price sensitivity.

- If all things are logically equal, the emotional connection will win the sale.

- Making an emotional connection protects your company from criticism.

Further reading:

- **Fisk, P. (2008)** *Business Genius,* **Capstone Press**

- **Gladwell, M. (2005)** *Blink: The Power of Thinking without Thinking,* **Penguin**

- **Stratten, S. (2010)** *UnMarketing: Stop Marketing. Start Engaging,* **John Wiley & Sons**

- **Tovey, D. (2012)** *Principled Selling: How to Win More Business Without Selling Your Soul,* **Kogan Page**

Their pace = your timing

A person's time is precious. It's their gift to allow you time to tell them about your offer. So, whilst the right timing is important to catch someone when they're in a buying frame of mind, earning the right to take up a person's time is critical. This is especially true if you want to build long-term customer relationships.

The right to time

It's no secret that effective timing is an essential ingredient of successful marketing. Spotting seasonality and maintaining frequency are the easy things to manage. Getting people to *want*

> *Getting people to want to spend time with you is more of a challenge.*

to spend time with you is more of a challenge. To pull people through the buying decision, you need to understand how much time they want to give to the process. Then, ensure that you have the right tools and techniques of an appropriate duration, available when they want them.

Grabbing someone's attention is something that's done in seconds. A person will either notice you, or they won't. Then the moment has passed. As they then start to consider buying from you, they will gradually increase the time that they're happy to devote to finding out about your products and services.

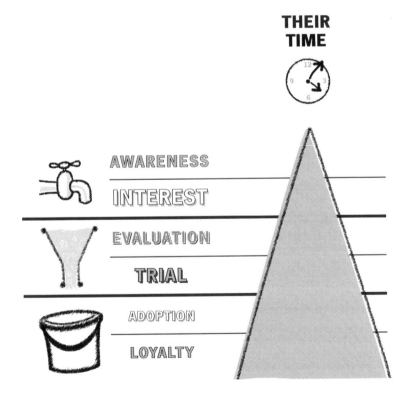

THEIR TIME

AWARENESS

INTEREST

EVALUATION

TRIAL

ADOPTION

LOYALTY

Leading on from the discussion in chapter three about your messages, it's easy to see that emotional triggers get intuitive and instinctive responses, which means they're quick. As the logical brain kicks in the processes become far more conscious and considered, and take more time.

You'll also find that the greater the risk or value of the purchase, the longer the buying process. This is not least because people feel they need to *show* that they're giving the decision proper attention. In professional buying, this is called due diligence. But, it doesn't only happen in business. The interesting thing about this phenomenon is that even if a person has already completely emotionally bought-in to the purchase, they will often slow themselves (or someone around them) down to show that they're not being rash.

> *They will often slow themselves down to show that they're not being rash.*

I recently bought a new handbag. It wasn't cheap. I went into the store looking for something quite different, and the bag caught my eye. I immediately loved it and had all but decided to buy it before looking at the price tag. I then proceeded to show it to my husband, and on the 20-minute walk around the store I rattled off how it would go with so many different outfits, it would fit my laptop and work books which meant I could use it for work and casual; I pointed out the high-quality stitching suggesting that it would last – I even had a stab at working out how much it would cost per use over the next six months or so. Now, let's be clear – my husband didn't care whether I bought the bag or not, it's my money, and my decision. I wasn't seeking approval from him; I was seeking approval from *me*. By taking the time to demonstrate (and externally validate) the logic of my purchase, I could justify my emotional desire to have it. And, this was for a purchase nearer the impulse end of the spectrum. Which goes to show that whatever you're selling, you need to give people the time and space to run this process.

To secure more, and more profitable, sales your marketing needs to take the emotional and logical messages you've just looked at, and deliver them in steadily increasing time chunks across the buying decision. If you nail this you will steadily earn the right to a person's precious time.

Match their schedule

You'll need to work out what amount of time your buyers want to give to this process, and then design materials or activities of about that duration. Put yourself in their position and think about how you would go through the buying decision. Consider the likely blocks of time they would have in their day for thinking about it. For a non-work purchase this is likely to be over a cup of tea, in a lunch break, on the journey to work, in the evening in front of the TV, or at the weekend. For a professional buying decision, it's worth thinking about the way that people typically chunk their work diaries – for example, 30 minute or 1 hour meetings. And, it's worth thinking about what you can do to help them make better use of a hectic schedule. Can you find ways of fitting a little information into those 'times in between', like 5 minutes before a meeting, whilst travelling, etc? Now, map this against the stages in a typical buying decision:

- How long might you have to grab their attention?

- If they're casually interested, how long will they give it?

- If they're starting to evaluate what you do, how long?

- How long might they give you to demonstrate or explain your products?

- How long might they spend reading a detailed proposal before approving it?

For my marketing consultancy business, this looks something like this, over a 6 to 12 week period:

Their step	Their time	Think...
AWARENESS	<10 seconds	See a Tweet, click on it
INTEREST	<5 minutes	Read a blog article
EVALUATION	<20 minutes	Read a service page and watch a case study video
TRIAL	<60 minutes	Attend an online seminar
	<90 minutes	First meeting
ADOPTION	<90 minutes	Read proposal
	2 days	Undertake Audit
LOYALTY	Ongoing relationship	Convert into 12-month client

Getting your timing wrong can scupper your sale. If your buyer has 5 minutes, but all you have available to them is a densely packed product guide that would take 20 minutes to read, you've lost them. And, if you have a competitor who got to the point more quickly, it's highly likely that this buyer is now considering their offer, not yours.

Having an idea of the different time blocks your buyer is likely to want to give to their decision allows you to create appropriate tools and materials to meet this. Most businesses already have lots of great material, it's just not cut up into the right chunks. You'll hear people talk about bite-sized chunks. But, if someone wants a meal, you need to give them one. That is, if they want to really interrogate your offering, you need to have all the information they would want available. They just may not want it all in one sitting.

Most businesses already have lots of great material, it's just not cut up into the right chunks.

Let's consider how you might present a case study across a buying decision. A case study is not one item – it's a piece of content that needs to be split into appropriate chunks:

Their step	Their time	Case study presented as
AWARENESS	<10 seconds	100 character one-liners to use as Tweets or social media status updates
INTEREST	<5 minutes	A 3-minute client interview video
EVALUATION	<20 minutes	A page of web copy with more detail
TRIAL	<60 minutes	A downloadable version with more detail Perhaps included in a web seminar
ADOPTION	<90 minutes	Slides with key facts and figures to include in a presentation at your first meeting
LOYALTY	Ongoing relationship	A version sent to existing customers in similar businesses highlighting any service areas they're not currently using

If you've worked out the likely durations your buyers spend at each stage of the process, you now need to take a look at your marketing materials to see if you can slice them up accordingly. This is much more effective than putting everything in one place and expecting your buyers to look at it all at once. By breaking up your materials you allow your buyer to:

- Reach the right messages at the right time

- Digest what they need to in the time they have available

- Feel like they are giving the decision due attention

- Dip into different materials over an extended period of time.

An integrated marketing campaign will have something of each duration to take people through the whole journey.

In your workbook

- Your buyers' schedule

- How long will they give it?

Sell the next step

Having this gradual increase in time investment through the process allows the buyer to move at their own pace. Some people may race through this process. Others may take a little longer. Enabling the buyer to move from one step to the next at their own pace gives them the sense of control. They feel invited into the decision, rather than bombarded. Separating the steps, and the materials you use to support them, also allows you to hit the right emotional and logical notes along the way.

> *Enabling the buyer to move from one step to the next at their own pace gives them the sense of control.*

The key to making this work is to make sure that one step leads to the next. You need to leave the buyer wanting a little more at each stage, and signposting where they can get it. The key words in that last sentence are 'a little more' – don't jump the gun. If someone has just read a blog post, it's unlikely that they're ready to buy, so emblazoning a massive 'buy now' button isn't quite right. Signposting a related service is. And, from that service page, signposting a case study detailing someone using that particular service is spot on.

Getting this 'next step' signposting right is often the Achilles' heel in a marketing set-up. Take a look at your materials: is there always an option for the buyer to get that *one* step more, or are you asking them to leapfrog straight to calling you to arrange a meeting when they've just started on their journey?

Having an integrated set of time-chunked materials mapped out is also highly beneficial for your team. Having the different pieces of information gives your people reasons to get back in touch with buyers as they go through the process.

It also means that your marketing materials act like an additional member, or members, of your team with a job to do. At the top of the process, the job is to qualify potential buyers. If you get this right and a potential buyer exits the process before you actually talk to them, you can see this as a positive. If you've presented highly relevant and compelling material, but they decided not to take it any further – then they almost certainly weren't going to buy. If the stepping stones hadn't been there and you would previously have had a phone call or sales meeting with that person, you can consider your time saved. This is valuable time that can now be redirected to talking to people who are more likely to buy. The idea is that your marketing stepping stones do a great deal of the sales qualification, meaning that your best people are being used for best effect.

If you've presented highly relevant and compelling material, but they decided not to take it any further – then they almost certainly weren't going to buy.

CASE STUDY: Conscious Solutions

Conscious Solutions provides digital marketing and web services to law firms in the UK. They have a total commitment to 'next step' selling. In a recent campaign their Tap was LinkedIn advertisements directing people to a simple booklet download. The 'next step' was simply to get people to agree to a product demonstration. The LinkedIn campaign ran for three months and generated 1,309 clicks, at a cost of £3,636. From this they secured 127 booklet downloads. From amongst these people Conscious Solutions has delivered £35,050 in revenue within twelve months and has another £22,280 in forecast. For every campaign they run, or inbound enquiry they receive from other sources, the Conscious Solutions team has mapped an ideal 'next step'. David Gilroy, Sales & Marketing Director, comments, "I don't doubt that if we had jumped straight in to trying to secure a sales meeting with these 127 people we would have burned their permission. Even if enquiries come into the business seemingly pre-sold, we will always only sell them the next step because I've found that if you do so, you get many more people to follow the whole path."

The ZigZag

What you'll find with most considered purchases, is that engagement with your materials or activities doesn't happen in one sitting. Even those that seem to happen at speed, usually do so after an extended period of zigzagging around the top of the process.

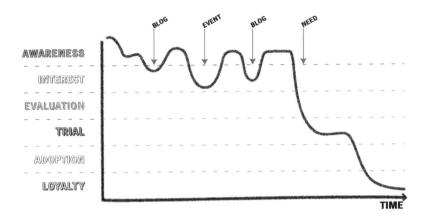

They might casually hear about you and read a blog post. Then, because they're not looking for what you have at the moment, they'll simply file your company in the 'mildly interesting' part of their brain. They might then see a speaker of yours at an event and think the talk was really useful and sign up to receive your newsletter. Sometimes they'll open it, sometimes they'll click on an article. People might do this for months, or even years, until one day they have a need for what you offer, at which point they turn straight to you and power through their buying decision. You need to facilitate this zigzag. You need to allow people to dip in and out of your material, and pop up at regular intervals to prompt them to do so.

 Because people float around the top of this process for a period of time, you need a steady stream of new and interesting materials to keep this going. What this means in practice is that the tools that work further down the buying process need refreshing less frequently. An annual or biannual refresh of the deeper pieces might be complemented by a rolling programme of marketing content at daily, weekly, monthly and quarterly intervals.

Their step	Their time	Possible tools
AWARENESS	<10 seconds	• Daily Social Media interaction
INTEREST	<5 minutes	• Weekly blog post • Monthly subscriber newsletter
EVALUATION	<20 minutes	• Quarterly paper and/or web seminar
TRIAL	<60 minutes	• Sales meeting (core content refreshed six-monthly)
ADOPTION	As appropriate	• Gateway Product (e.g. Audit: refreshed annually) • On-boarding communications across a Welcome Window
LOYALTY	Ongoing relationship	• All of the above as part of a customer communications programme • Annual customer forum or hospitality event

In addition to this steady flow of marketing activities, you'll also need to plan and make use of the seasonality of your market. This is covered in chapter eight.

 Think of ways to cut up and re-purpose your marketing content to give it a longer shelf life.

CASE STUDY: ShipServ

Keeping people engaged in conversation was a primary
concern for ShipServ, an online marketplace for the maritime
industry. A key tool for this was a monthly email newsletter.
To increase subscriptions and to have a little fun with their
audience, they ran a competition to name the newsletter. This
received over 200 responses. John Watton, then marketing
director, filmed a short piece to camera in which he read out
each suggestion, overdubbed with humorous quotes. This,
together with other light-hearted video content, gave them a
library of video snippets to feed out via social media and email.
The videos were also perfect for their audience to pass on
themselves, which increased the reach and generated a number
of additional subscribers. This activity provided content for use
over a number of weeks, raising and maintaining Awareness
in that time. It also secured a number of new subscribers, who
then went on to receive the newsletter each month.

Slow down to sell more

Making sure you have clear stepping stones can often be seen as
slowing the sale down. This can seem counterintuitive to anyone
who wants to see sales results, fast.

There's an approach to selling that's always gunning for the close.
There's an almost macho desire to get to a deal in the shortest
time possible. This is particularly true when you talk to salespeople
who need to hit a time-based target to secure commission. Indeed,
for many, securing a quick sale shows their skill.
However, for long-term sales results, this approach
doesn't work. It can be a really hard habit to break.
But, if you do, you'll reap the rewards. Go at your
buyers' pace and you'll achieve higher average order
values and keep customers longer.

> There's an almost macho desire to get to a deal in the shortest time possible.

You need to adopt a nurtured approach in which you earn the right to their time. You need to give them time and space to think, and the materials they need to proactively choose a relationship with your business. It's about ensuring that when they do buy from you they are fully committed to their purchase. In many sales-driven businesses this means that you need to slow your sales

You shouldn't be pushing them onto it, it's more like offering a helping hand to steady their step as they choose to go forward.

down. Or, at least, you should not be afraid to do so if that's what the buyer wants. That's not to say you can't be proactive in putting a compelling stepping stone in front of them. But, you shouldn't be pushing them onto it, it's more like offering a helping hand to steady their step as they choose to go forward.

It's fair to ask about people who come to you already part-way through their buying decision. If you've worked hard in fostering your referrer relationships, this should be happening. When it does, potential buyers can seem to come to you halfway down this process, or pre-sold. Beware! You need to be absolutely sure that they really have done the thinking, because if they haven't done so before the sale, they will do so afterwards. You can't, and shouldn't try, to shortcut the psychology. It doesn't really matter at what point in the process they hand over their cash, the mind will always run over the same ground. You shouldn't put *unnecessary* hurdles in their way, but you should give them the opportunity to run through the steps of a considered purchase in full before you take their money. If you've not really secured Adoption when they pay you, the risk of losing the customer before you make any profit is much higher. It may be as simple as sending them a helpful paper, or pointing them to a relevant blog post, rather than piling in with your prices and product information. Jump in too soon and you could either lose the sale entirely, make a sale that bounces, or end up with less value from it than was possible. Put simply, slower sales stick.

Prepare talking points for inbound enquiries that help you assess where they are in their thinking and what material to point them to depending on their answers.

CASE STUDY: KashFlow

KashFlow, providers of online accounting software for small businesses, exhibited at business events in their early days. They took experienced salespeople and targetted them on sign-ups secured on the day. Initially, this seemed highly effective. However, within days the customer service team was receiving calls from people who'd got back to their desks and changed their minds. It takes roughly eight months for KashFlow to break even on their average cost of customer acquisition, so customers who defect this early really aren't worth having. Chief Executive, Duane Jackson comments, "We never push for a close any more. We believe that if we answer their questions, and our software suits them, they'll sign up in their own time." Since moving away from hard sell techniques to a wholly service-oriented model, with no salespeople at all, with the whole emphasis on simply being helpful and friendly, their retention levels have settled at around 90% year-on-year. And, being as roughly 10% of businesses in their target market go under each year, you could argue that this represents almost non-existent customer defection.

Getting into a slower sales habit is a lot to do with values. It can mean re-assessing the way you recruit, train and reward your sales team. It could even mean changing your perception of what a sales team is. In some businesses, the people that buyers really want to deal with in the sales process are the people that they'll deal with as a customer. So, it may actually be better for sales to be a core skill that is integrated into everyone's role rather being seen as a distinct function. Either way, long-term relationships are much more likely when each party is genuinely useful to the other. If you can shift the mindset of your business to one of being genuinely helpful to people, rather than selling to them, you'll reap the rewards. Hard sell techniques rarely work a second time. So, unless your business model is to only ever sell someone something once, then it's worth remembering that softer, slower, sales will last longer and net more both in their own right and in their impact on your wider reputation.

One of the quickest ways to start changing sales behaviour is to look at the way people are paid. If they're on a monthly target, for example, it can be very tempting for them to try to shortcut the process. Linking performance rewards to a stepped process can really help. A key measure to add into any sales remuneration is a measure of the quality, as defined by such things as how long they stay a customer, their additional purchases over time, and their referral value. You certainly shouldn't be paying out commission until a new customer has covered their own cost of acquisition. These sorts of performance measures should start to weed out any hard sell.

 Review your sales remuneration package to reward sales nurturing as well as completing the first deal.

CASE STUDY: Ovation Finance

Ovation Finance, a team of independent financial advisers, have structured their bonus scheme to include relationship nurturing activities. As well as rewarding income generated, each adviser earns points linked to simple client communication activities, such as picking up the phone to see how they're doing. Managing Director, Chris Budd, comments, "One of our competitors used to run an internal competition where the highest earning adviser each month got to drive a Ferrari. In the year they ran this activity they made record profits. In the following year, they went bust. I don't doubt that these two things were linked as the hard sell techniques came back to bite. I want our advisers to give good advice and build relationships with clients that bring a steady income in the long term, so that's exactly what we reward." Ovation has secured consistent year-on-year growth, and last year 92% of their income came from amongst their existing clients.

Be quick about it

You may well find that slowing sales down is highly beneficial. But, that doesn't mean that you don't need to be quick about it. A person may take months of nurturing to finally ask you a question. When they do, you need to get back to them quickly. Being responsive at each point that the potential buyer requests anything from you is absolutely key. There's an increasing expectation of immediacy, particularly if yours is an online business, or someone is contacting you via a social or digital channel. At each stage you should be inviting conversation. Conversation is two-way and in the moment. You must have systems in place that allow you to respond to people quickly because you want to get back to them whilst the question is still relevant and before one of your competitors does.

You want to get back to them whilst the question is still relevant and before one of your competitors does.

Set internal service-level-agreements on how long it will take you to respond to inbound enquiries. Think about how you respond outside normal office hours.

Time to plan

Engagement with different time bound pieces is also an extremely useful indicator as to where people are in the journey. For example, if you know that someone has downloaded a how-to guide that would take more than 20 minutes to read, or attended an hour-long web seminar, you can assume that they're pretty interested in what you do. Armed with this information, your business is better able to predict and prepare for future demand. This means that you're much more able to live up to, or even exceed, customer expectations. A poorly planned promotion can have a devastating effect on a business. There's nothing worse than generating loads of demand, but not being able to fulfil it. Not only do you miss out on that potential business, but poor experience and disappointment can lead to negative word of mouth that is damaging in the long term. If you have a way of slowing the sales down, by Funneling them through a Gateway Offer for example, you can stay ahead of demand – which might mean recruitment, training, upping production, etc. In a small business, you can do this in a simple spreadsheet. For larger operations, or more complex businesses, online or hosted tools are available for a low monthly fee to help you do this.

> *There's nothing worse than generating loads of demand, but not being able to fulfil it.*

 Build, or use an existing tool, that gives you a view of your sales pipeline so that you can plan for the forthcoming demand.

After a period of tracking engagement with your different materials, you'll be able to determine what proportion of people who demonstrate interest in your company eventually buy from you. If you're really smart, you'll be able to determine over what approximate time period. By providing opportunities for buyers to engage with your business in increasing time chunks, you can measure the numbers of people giving extended periods of time to considering your offering. Even if you can't see this on an individual level, you should be able to see movement. Putting this information together means that you'll know how many people you'll need to be engaging with your short materials now in order to meet your sales targets in, say, six months time. Marketing measurement, and using it for planning and refinement, is covered more in chapter ten.

In your workbook

- What comes next?

- Slow it down

- Ready to respond?

Key points

- You need to earn the right to take up a person's time.

- Think of ways to help people rather than sell to them.

- Cut your material into chunks of time that increase in duration through the buying decision.

- Reward long-term sales results more than you reward the speed of a first sale.

- Build in rewards for nurturing buyer relationships.

- Use your marketing materials to qualify potential buyers.

- Only ever sell the 'next step'.

- Respond quickly when someone enquires.

- Have enough fresh content to enable people to stay interested for a period of time.

- Use interactions with different materials as indicators of future business so that you can be ready for it.

Further reading:

- **Jefferson, S. and Tanton, S. (2013)** *Valuable Content Marketing: How to Make Quality Content the Key to Your Business Success,* **Kogan Page**

- **Stratten, S. (2010)** *UnMarketing: Stop Marketing. Start Engaging,* **John Wiley & Sons**

- **Tovey, D. (2012)** *Principled Selling: How to Win More Business Without Selling Your Soul,* **Kogan Page**

Their team = your audiences

Buying decisions, particularly high-value or complex ones, are not made in isolation. An enthusiast might spend time on a forum and reading reviews, a husband might ask his wife and children, and an employee might ask colleagues or their boss. In many cases gaining the input, and approval, of others is essential in the buying decision. You need to know who your buyers are talking to, and get those people on side. You need to know who's on their team, and get them on yours.

The decision team

 The source of a message is often as important as the message itself. The opinions of others are sought during a buying decision for two main reasons: people may wish to shortcut the process by asking someone they think knows the subject well, and secondly, they may look for reassurance that their decision is sound.

 This is why you'll hear marketers talk about including 'influencers' as part of your wider audience. It's good advice. But, it's such a broad term. Thinking about which specific people have what level of influence at each stage of the process allows you to communicate with them more precisely.

What's interesting, and powerful in terms of your marketing, is to think about the different people buyers turn to at the different stages of their decision. What you'll typically find is that people cast the net wide in the early stages and then reduce down the people whose opinion they particularly value as they get closer to the purchase.

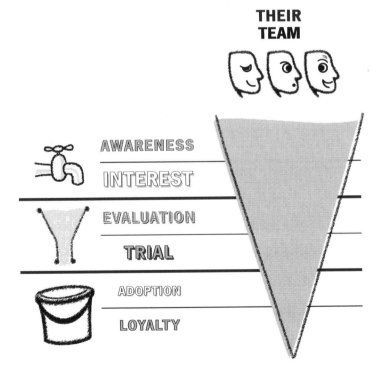

In practice the extended buying team involved in a considered purchase might look like this:

Their step	Who?	For example
AWARENESS	Word of mouth	People they follow on social media
INTEREST	Influencers	People seen as experts on the subject
EVALUATION	Referrers	People they actually know
TRIAL	Decision makers	People affected by the decision
ADOPTION	Buyers	People who could veto the decision
LOYALTY	Users	People who use what's bought

 Go through this list and work up a description of who these people are. Include job titles, gender, media consumption, social status, etc.

For some businesses your users might be a larger pool. For example, a large software implementation might be bought by a small buying team but used by hundreds of people on rollout. If this is the case in your business, your sketch for their team will flare out at the bottom to look a little like an ice cream sundae glass.

Let me walk you through how I found my accountant as an example:

My steps	Who I asked...	My sources
AWARENESS	I put out a Tweet and a LinkedIn status update asking connections in my area if they knew of any good local accountants.	Across these platforms there are well over 1000 people in my local area who could have replied.
INTEREST	Across the two platforms, 20 people replied with suggestions.	20

My steps	Who I asked...	My sources
EVALUATION	I looked up the suggested accountants on LinkedIn, and found 5 where I could see that someone I knew seemed to be connected to someone at the accountants. I picked up the phone to those 5 people and asked what they were like, and reduced it to 3.	5
TRIAL	I looked at their websites, and then called the 3 recommended accountants and had a phone conversation. From this, I asked to meet with 1 of them.	3
ADOPTION	My husband joined me at the meetings, and we jointly decided who to go with.	2 (my husband and the shortlisted accountant)
LOYALTY	I now maintain my relationship with my accountant without reference to any third parties.	1

At the beginning I asked around without much selectivity. As the decision drew closer, I relied on sources I really trusted to help me with this decision. To a greater or lesser extent, your buyers will be doing the same. This is partly because there's a limit to what can be reasonably asked of friends, family and colleagues in terms of the time they'll give to helping with the decision. But, it's also because the opinion of some people matters more than others.

The opinion of some people matters more than others.

Who needs to know what?

To be able to appropriately affect your buyers' influencers, you need to identify who they are and map them against the decision making process. This allows you to focus your attention on key people, and to work out the specific types of information those people should be exposed to. By noting the stage in the process at which they're likely to be asked their opinion, you'll now be able to map the appropriate message content based on the needs at each stage from chapter three, and likely time duration these people might give also to the process from chapter four.

The point is that not everyone needs (or wants) to know everything. For example, at Awareness you simply need to be a name that comes to mind, but at Evaluation a referrer might be expected to have an idea of the other clients you work with. Here's roughly what the different people need to know about you:

Their step	Who?	They need to know...
AWARENESS	Word of mouth	Your company name and broad area of expertise
INTEREST	Influencers	Rough idea of what you do
EVALUATION	Referrers	That you're good at what you do
TRIAL	Decision makers	The practical detail they need to make their decision
ADOPTION	Buyers	What it will be like to work with you
LOYALTY	Users	Everything they need to work well with you

With the explosion in social media, it is now easier than ever to find your buyers' extended team; for example:

- You can find their colleagues on LinkedIn or similar sites.

- You can see what groups they are a member of on LinkedIn.

- You can see who they are following on Twitter, YouTube, etc.

- You can see material they've bookmarked, shared and favourited.

 Get every customer-facing person in your business trained on researching people in social media.

 In your workbook

- Who's on their team?

- Buying team message map

Reaching third parties

Having identified and categorised their team, you now need to go about getting them on yours. This is where networking and word of mouth really matters. It's not just who your buyer is connected to that counts, but who they're connected to, and so on.

CASE STUDY: Connect Assist

When Patrick Nash, Chief Executive of Connect Assist, was looking for expert advice on their marketing strategy, he decided to shortcut the process by asking someone he trusted: his chairman. However, his chairman couldn't think of anyone. He, in turn, picked up the phone to a public relations professional he trusted. She said that advising on the wider marketing strategy wasn't what she did, but to let her think about it. She logged onto LinkedIn and performed an 'advanced search' on the term 'marketing strategy' within 10km of her office. She looked at the websites of the people who came up, and enquired with a few of them and introduced the ones she felt was most appropriate to Patrick. Following submission of a proposal and a number of meetings, the company that was found via a search on LinkedIn won the business.

What this case study shows is that when it comes to social media, the people buying your stuff don't necessarily need to be actively engaged in it themselves for it to have a powerful effect on their buying decision. This is particularly true in selling to Boards and to families. In the boardroom, it's unlikely that the Chief Executive is going to be constantly plugged into Twitter or avidly consuming blog content. But, as the task to research a

> *When it comes to social media, the people buying your stuff don't necessarily need to be actively engaged in it themselves for it to have a powerful effect on their buying decision.*

given purchase is often passed down the line, it is increasingly likely that someone else that they ask is. In families, parents might not spend hours poring over review sites to choose their next family holiday – but a teenage child might well do. In my house, I certainly won't spend time on a gadgetry forum before buying a new TV, but my husband wouldn't think of buying electronics without doing so.

 Make sure your company, and people, show up in these sorts of searches.

The Connect Assist case study also demonstrates that in most circumstances putting all your eggs in an online basket probably won't enable you to reach everyone you'd like to. Go back to the last table, and now add an indication of their media consumption. This will help you to work out where you might need to be targetting your content and messaging to get picked up by the right people.

There are systems available these days that allow you to apply Influencer scores to your marketing database or email list. This can highlight groups of people with whom you may want to communicate differently. For example, giving them early access to new product information or inviting them to your events. These sorts of metrics, like Klout and PeerIndex, typically rely on a person's social media activity and can be helpful in generating word of mouth for your business. It's also worth remembering, of course, that there are highly influential people who never use social media, and some highly questionable people who obsess about their scoring. Judgement is always needed when relying on a score that's worked out by an algorithm.

> *There are highly influential people who never use social media, and some highly questionable people who obsess about their scoring.*

CASE STUDY: Valuable Content

Content marketing specialists, Valuable Content, gain the majority of their business through referrals and collaborations with other marketing suppliers. To ensure that this source is maintained, they take care to keep referrers engaged with their materials. Sonja Jefferson, Managing Director, comments, "Our new posts are, of course, promoted in social media and to email subscribers, but I also drop a personal note to key contacts to whom I believe it would be of interest. I specifically ask them for their feedback." This puts the content in front of their advocates, keeping them engaged and alerting them to new material that they might pass on to others. It also triggers a number of considered comments, which in turn kicks off dialogue. Since initiating this additional personal touch to their activity, Valuable Content has seen comments and sharing of their blog material double.

Having communications or tools that are aimed specifically at different sets of people is extremely effective. Specific appropriate techniques for buyers, and their extended teams, are provided in Part Three.

Consider including social events in your calendar to which you invite key third parties.

Bearing all of this in mind, it's worth taking another look at your marketing database, contacts list or little black book. People you may previously have thought of as 'hangers on' may not have immediate value in terms of being a buyer themselves. But, they could certainly already be, or later become, an influencer of others.

In your workbook

- What media do they consume?

- Social media research checklist

- Get found in social media

- Getting the word out

The internal salesperson

Of all of these third parties, people with the power of veto are arguably the most important. In many cases you will be one step removed from the all-important conversation with the critical third party. That is, your buyer (not you) needs to convince and seek the approval of others to move forward with the decision. They need to become your salesperson.

In a business setting, this might mean the finance director signing off on a proposal. In a family setting it might mean spousal agreement, as we saw in Leak #5. You still have a role here, which is to equip your buyer to sell your ideas internally. When the objective is to get your buyer to convince others of the validity of their buying decision, it can be powerful to create marketing materials aimed specifically at the third party. And, if your budget is limited, reaching these critical third parties probably needs to be the focus of any influencer marketing.

Brainstorm all the reasons someone would say no to another person's request to buy your products and services. Address them.

In your workbook

- Reasons to say no

Your Commercial Karma

 Where you might create specific materials for people with a power of veto, it's often non-marketing communication that informs the opinion of other third parties. Keeping the wider buying team in mind is a powerful reminder of why it's important to treat people well in business. As we saw in Leak #11, nobody is nobody. Anyone you come into contact with could be an important influencer.

Think about:

- Employees, unsuccessful job applicants, ex-employees

- Customers, ex-customers, people who enquired but didn't buy

- Suppliers, ex-suppliers, companies that tendered for your business but didn't get it

- Your competitors – or people in a similar industry.

It can be very tempting to think of competitors, in particular, as the enemy. And, as such, to want to lock down all of your information to hide it from them. Of course, as a business owner and someone who puts a lot of intellectual property out there, I can whole-heartedly understand this sentiment. But, competitors are often very important to the long-term health of your business.

 For my part, I figure that there are enough business speaking, writing and consulting opportunities for the world to need more than one person (or company) that does the sort of thing I do. What's more, we've seen how removing some potential buyers from your sales process can sometimes be the best thing for your business. So, it's well worth having a list of people you would hand them on to. This should be done with real professional dignity. Don't hand someone on because you think they're going to be a problem client and you want to spite your

Don't hand someone on because you think they're going to be a problem client and you want to spite your competitor.

competitor. Pass people on to people you think are a good fit. The prospect may come back one day in the right shape for your business. Or, because of how honest and decent you were, they may recommend you to others. The competitor might also reciprocate, pointing clients with a better fit for your company in your direction. And, of course, in any good competitor, there's your next fantastic recruit. So, all in all, it's well worth keeping competitors on your horizon as worthwhile influencers.

How you, and all of the people and systems in your business, conduct themselves will become the footprint you leave. This will be happening whether you're actively aware of it or not. Taking some time to consider, and therefore affect, the legacy of each interaction can help you to ensure that whomever your buyer turns to, they will have something good to say about you. This is even more important if these people are visibly connected to you in some way. For example, they are a contact of yours, or one of your employees, on a social network. I regularly look people up on LinkedIn, then pick up the phone to a common connection to find out more about them. You can be sure that I'm not the only one.

So, as well as thinking about how you deal with the people in direct contact with your business, think about those to whom you are indirectly linked. For example, ensuring that all job applicants receive a letter of thanks for their application, and all short-listed candidates are offered constructive feedback on their interview. The same is true of suppliers. If you've been on the receiving end of an unsuccessful tender, you'll know how important it is to have the effort you put in recognised, and the reasons for the knock-back explained. The ultimate outcome of this action is to leave everyone who comes into contact with your business with a good opinion of it. Treating people decently in this way will build up goodwill – call it Commercial Karma. And, goodwill in business (as in life) always comes back to you with interest.

> *Treating people decently in this way will build up goodwill – call it Commercial Karma.*

Review the communications that go to all people in recruitment or pitch processes to ensure that it is helpful and friendly.

CASE STUDY: Ovation Finance

Ovation Finance, independent financial advisors (IFA), was recently contacted by a partner in a local law firm. She was a good friend of one of the Ovation team and had heard a lot about the business. Her firm had a list of companies to whom they would refer business, and a slot on the list had become available for an IFA. Having heard so much from her trusted friend, they were the first company that came to mind to go on the list. Having looked at their website, and been impressed with the materials she was happy to recommend them as their referral partner. Chris Budd, Managing Director at Ovation Finance, comments, "I was delighted that a respected local firm wanted to refer business our way; I was even more delighted that it had come about by virtue of a happy member of my team chatting to a friend. That's how business really happens."

 In your workbook

- Company communications checklist
- Who are you connected to?

Key points

- Buyers talk to different people at different stages in their decision.

- They cast the net wide, then reduce their focus to key trusted people as the decision draws near.

- Different people need to know different things about your business.

- Think about the media consumption of the third parties, not just the buyer.

- Be particularly alert to people with the power of veto.

- Think of ways to equip your buyer to become an internal salesperson.

- Consider the legacy all of your interactions.

Further reading:

- **Scott, D. M. (2010) 2nd ed.** *The New Rules of Marketing & PR,* **John Wiley & Sons**

- **Townsend, H. (2011)** *FT Guide to Business Networking: How to Use the Power of Online and Offline Networking for Business Success,* **Pearson**

- **Tovey, D. (2012)** *Principled Selling: How to Win More Business Without Selling Your Soul,* **Kogan Page**

SUMMARY OF PART TWO

Looking at a purchasing decision from a buyer's perspective helps you to understand the information they are looking for, the time they have available and the people they trust to help them with their choices. There is no such thing as a killer marketing message. What you need is an interlinked series of messages that start with emotion, move on to logic and then return to emotion – The Logic Sandwich.

Digesting this information from the businesses that a person has on their list to consider takes time. And, a person's time is a precious resource. You need to earn the right to it. You do this by being genuinely helpful and fitting in with their busy lives.

Because time is so precious, people will often try to shortcut the process by asking others to do a little of the thinking for them. They will ask for suggestions, recommendations and even permission from people they already trust. Gaining the respect of those third parties can make or break your sale.

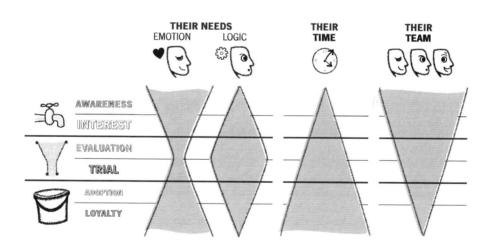

MEET VA-VOOM!

Virtual Assistants. Real Potential.

To really bring the ideas in this book to life, you'll now be following the progress of an imaginary company, VA-Voom!, as they put a Watertight Marketing operation in place for their business.

VA-Voom! is a small business offering Virtual Assistant services. There are two founders who act as joint managing directors. They've been in business three years, employ 15 people, and turnover just over £1m per annum.

They provide secretarial and administrative support over the phone and online. They do the sorts of things that a personal assistant would do, for example:

- Diary management, travel arrangements, etc.

- Telephone answering

- Dictation, proofreading and document formatting

- Website updates, social media management, marketing administration.

In addition to these services, they also provide packaged training and templates for key administrative activities, and run an annual conference on productivity and personal effectiveness.

There are three key groups of people for whom their products and services are useful:

- Small business owners, sole traders and freelancers

- Directors and senior managers in larger businesses without access to administrative support

- People running one-off large projects or with peaks in administrative requirements looking for overflow support.

Services can be paid for in the following ways:

- A monthly package of hours, with a minimum three-month contract. The more hours, the lower the hourly rate.

- A prepay account at a higher hourly rate that can be topped up at any time.

- A bespoke project or overflow support contract.

Growth strategy

The VA-Voom! founders are proud of the business they've built. It's grown organically and they now feel ready to step things up. They've set themselves an ambitious target of doubling the size of their business in revenue terms in the next two years.

They have set the target of upping their monthly personal subscriptions from 160 customers paying an average of £350 per month, to 225 customers paying an average of £425 per month. This takes annual revenue against this offering from £672,000 to £1,147,500. We will follow the marketing plan they put together to meet this target. The remainder of the growth will be made amongst corporate contracts, template sales, one-off projects and events.

To help them with this, they got themselves a copy of Watertight Marketing, and downloaded the Workbook. The two founders took a week out of the business to work through it and draw up an outline plan. They then kicked off a strategic initiative internally. The first phase was an intensive review and action plan to systematically address the Thirteen Touchpoint Leaks. The whole team was involved. Depending on workload, each member of the team was able to give between 10-20% of their working week for 12 weeks to get the groundwork done. In addition, each of the founders gave it 50% of their time for that concentrated period. So, in total, that was a time investment of 70 hours up front from the founders, a further 210 hours of their time over the 12-week period, and 63 hours from the rest of the team.

Here's a summary of what they put together mapped against the Watertight Marketing framework. You'll see more detail, and the rationale for these choices, as you read on.

Messaging

Buyers' step	Buyers' needs		VA-Voom! Key Messages
	Emotion	Logic	
AWARENESS	High	Low	Mundane tasks are holding you back from meeting your true potential.
INTEREST	Medium	Medium	• Are you on top of your to-do list, or is it on top of you? • Make time to meet your potential • Success means focussing on what you're good at
EVALUATION	Low	High	• Cost – *on average VA-Voom! clients get £70 of value from every hour we save them* • Speed – *tasks we're given are usually completed within just three hours, and we're available out of hours too* • Quality – *clients currently rate our service as 5/5 on all quality measures* • Functionality – *we've saved our busy clients over XXX hours this year* • Dependability – *client retention rates stand at over 80%* • This is how much time we could save you *(Time Saver Analyser)*
TRIAL	Low	High	• Find out if you're ready to make the most of a virtual assistant (*Time Saver Audit*) • Try the service at no risk with our one-month trial with money-back guarantee
ADOPTION	Medium	Medium	Let us free up the time you need to focus on meeting your true potential
LOYALTY	High	Low	What more can we do to help you meet your potential?

Toolkit

Buyers' step	Buyers' time	VA-Voom! Key Tools
AWARENESS	<10 seconds	• Daily updates on Twitter • Weekly updates on Linkedin • Monthly funny cartoon on Pinterest
INTEREST	<5 minutes	• Weekly blog posts on the VA-Voom! website • Monthly *Time Saver Tips* video • Monthly subscriber email newsletter • Case study videos • Key target direct mail • Affiliate Scheme with video tips
EVALUATION	<20 minutes	• Paper: *The Real Cost of Self-Administration* • Referral Scheme
TRIAL	<60 minutes	• Monthly web seminar: *Making time to meet your true potential* • Online Tool: *Time Saver Analyser*
ADOPTION	<6 Weeks	• One-month trial including the *Time Saver Audit* with money-back guarantee • Welcome Pack • Welcome Gift of an appropriate productivity / personal effectiveness book • 6-week on-boarding communications • Quarterly social events
LOYALTY	Ongoing relationship	• Customer satisfaction tracking • Customer version of newsletter • Discount vouchers for reviewed books • Annual client forum • Quarterly social events • Personalised client communication linked to enhanced data collection

This is supplemented with a *'Meet your true potential in 20XX'* campaign each January, and a set of appropriate seasonal activities and offers across the year.

Extended audience

Buyers' step	Buyers' team	VA-Voom! Audience
AWARENESS	Word of mouth	Anyone in a broadly office-based management role in the UK
INTEREST	Influencers	Business and management press, including: • Business pages of broadsheets • National magazines: Management Today, Director, Economist, etc. • Trade magazines: Growing Business, FSB's The Voice, etc. • Business Websites: SmartaHQ, BusinessZone, Startup Donut, FreelanceUK, etc. • Bloggers: key business bloggers talking to the same users.
EVALUATION	Referrers	Other companies providing services to these buyers, for example: Lawyers, Accountants, Business Consultants, Coaches, etc.
TRIAL	Decision makers	In large corporations the Human Resources and Finance teams often need to approve the use of a virtual assistant
ADOPTION	Buyers	Top 25 % of earners in the UK in roles that require self-administration
LOYALTY	Users	As above

Marketing-supported buyer journey

Buyers' step	Timeframe	What VA-Voom! does...
AWARENESS	Week 1	A potential buyer subscribes to the email newsletter. Sign-ups are usually as a result of their social media activity. When a person sign-ups they receive a beautifully-written welcome email that points them at further great content on the VA-Voom! website. One of the team receives a daily digest of any new email subscribers and undertakes initial research on them, from which they are categorised for follow-up.
INTEREST	Week 2	Any subscriber that has been flagged as a Tier 1 Prospect is allocated to a named assistant. This person would become their assistant if they were to take a contract. The VA-Voom! assistant then does some or all of the following, depending on their judgement: • Follows their prospect on social media, dropping them a note of thanks for subscribing to the newsletter and asking an appropriate friendly question • Follows their blog if they have one and leaves constructive comment if there's an opportunity to do so • Shares some of their content in social media if appropriate • Joins some of the same LinkedIn groups and follows the prospect's company on LinkedIn • Checks to see if they have any common connections in social media

Buyers' step	Timeframe	What VA-Voom! does...
EVALUATION	Week 3 to 4	If from this interaction they believe the prospect is a good fit for VA-Voom! the assistant: • Sends a copy of 'How to Save an Hour a Day' by Michael Heppell with a personalised letter and an invitation to attend the VA-Voom! web seminar *'Make time to meet your potential'*. • This is followed up by social media contact and a phone-call if appropriate.
TRIAL	Week 5 to 6	• The prospect is prompted to use the *Time Saver Analyser*, and to go on to the next step of undertaking the *Time Saver Audit*. • The one-month money-back trial is flagged from each of these steps, and personal follow-up is undertaken as appropriate.
ADOPTION	Week 6 to 10	• The buyer takes a one month trial and receives the Welcome Pack. • The assistant works with them during the trial, and a set of triggered emails is sent to guide them through making the most of the service.

Buyers' step	Timeframe	What VA-Voom! does...
LOYALTY	Week 10 to 16	• If they sign up beyond the trial, the VA-Voom! six-week 'Welcome Window' communications and satisfaction tracking kicks in.
	Ongoing...	• The customer is now switched to the customer version of the email newsletter, getting even more valuable content, a monthly competition to win the reviewed business book, invitations to quarterly social events and the annual VA-Voom! customer forum. • The assistant is trained in relationship nurturing, including how to spot up-sales and cross-sales opportunities and does so as appropriate.

The VA-Voom! Watertight Marketing 12-Month Plan, a range of fully worked sample marketing materials, and their completed Watertight Marketing Workbook are available to view and download from **watertightmarketing.com** website.

This company is entirely fictional. Any resemblance to real businesses, operational or defunct, is purely coincidental.

PART THREE

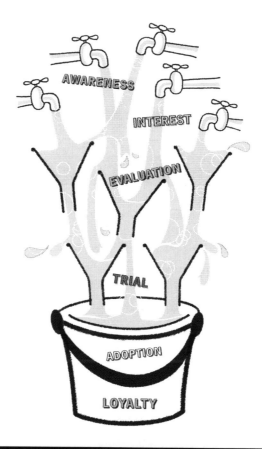

So far we've looked at the whole purchasing decision from your buyers' perspective. It's now time to look what you need to do about it. With their thinking firmly in mind, I'm now going to get really practical. I'm going to map the Thirteen Touchpoint Leaks against your Bucket, your Funnels and your Taps, and tell you exactly what to do about them. It's time to roll your sleeves up. It's time to fix those leaks – starting at the bottom!

BUCKET, FUNNELS AND TAPS

I want you to think of your offering, your product or your services, as a Bucket. This is where you collect customers. It's what keeps a customer happy with what they're buying from you. It's the area traditionally associated with customer service, but plugging the three identified marketing leaks across **Adoption** and **Loyalty** will ensure that you're not allowing good money to leak from your bottom line.

Then it's time to make sure you have those Funnels. In most organisations this best equates to your sales function. It's those things that you put in place to allow people to undertake an **Evaluation** of your offer, and **Trial** your company in order to convert their initial enquiry into a sale. There are a further three leaks to address here in terms of supporting the sales effort with the right marketing tools.

When you have these things in place, and only then, it's time to turn the Taps on. This is probably what most people think marketing is all about. That is, generating **Awareness** and stimulating **Interest** in what you have to sell. With seven leaks to address here, I can't imagine there are many companies who couldn't squeeze a little extra.

6

Your business Bucket

Filling a leaking Bucket is a fool's errand. There are already too many demands on your resources to risk leaking any precious funds unnecessarily. Keeping the customers you spent money acquiring is essential to making a profit. To do this you'll need to pay special attention to how the relationship starts, and to keeping them interested in what you do. The word 'relationship' is key. And, real relationships are based on an emotional connection. But, before all of that, you need to be sure that people want what you're selling.

Your Bucket relates to **Adoption** and **Loyalty**. It's all those things that come together to keep your customers your customers. There are three leaks to plug, and five questions to answer to make sure that your Bucket holds water.

Leak #1 – Forgotten customers – You need to keep your business front of your customers' minds, with close attention to:

- Your customer service – *are you available to help?*

- Your customer communications – *do you stay in touch?*

Leak #2 – Poor on-boarding – You need a systematic approach to welcoming new customers to ensure that they stay with you, by reviewing:

- Your Welcome Window – *do they get what they expected?*

Leak #3 – No emotional connection – You need a clear understanding of how to connect with your buyers on a human level, by looking at:

- Your brand or reputation – *what kind of people are you?*

But, before all of that you need to look at what you're selling:

- Your product or service offer – *do people want to buy what you're selling?*

There's a perpetual hole in your Bucket

Many businesses I've encountered will get in touch with a sales or marketing supplier thinking that what they need in this picture is more Taps. Seems reasonable. But, in the vast majority of cases, it's well worth addressing the Bucket for leaks first.

Think of your profit and loss account as a Bucket. A Bucket that will never be full. Water, here analogous with income, is a scarce resource and everybody is thirsty:

- There are your overheads and salaries to be paid each month.

- There's a certain level of inevitable wastage as customers stop buying (go out of business, leave the country, pass away, etc.).

- There's maintenance to be undertaken, capital investments, training, etc.

- There are taxes to be paid.

- And so on.

And, of course, the profit from your business is likely to be paid out to shareholders or directors, rather than simply accumulated. You'll need to keep that Bucket topped up to supply all those needs.

Your product or service offer

Do people want to buy what you're selling?

Being crystal clear about exactly what you do, and for whom, is key. Don't be tempted to think that you can build an offer that suits everyone. It simply isn't believable that you can be all things to all people. Managing directors who tell me that their services apply to anyone usually make me wonder if this means that they will often let everyone down. It's hard enough to get an offering right for a

It's hard enough to get an offering right for a well-defined audience, trying to offer a one-size-fits-all solution usually means that you expect everyone to wear a potato sack.

well-defined audience, trying to offer a one-size-fits-all solution usually means that you expect everyone to wear a potato sack. Even something that is as much of a commodity as toilet paper actually has quite clear market segments – like recycled for people with environmental concerns, coloured for people who like everything to match, quilted for... well let's not go there, but you can see what I mean. You need to find a large enough group of people with a similar need, to which you can address your offer.

Take the description of who you think your buyers are and conduct some research with your existing customers to verify any assumptions you've made.

WORKED EXAMPLE: VA-VOOM!

To get a real sense of the people using their services, they asked each of their assistants to give them a rundown on each of their clients. Specifically, things like age, gender, working life, family life, interests, earnings, and the likely information sources they might refer to. Pulling this information together, they determined that their clients had the following common characteristics:

- High-flying ambitious people

- Almost certainly in the top 25 % of earners in the UK

- Most clients were aged 30 or more

- Quite a high proportion had young families

- The gender mix was pretty balanced

- Working long hours, upwards of 50 hours per week into the evening and at weekends

- They have an 'always-on' mentality and usually have a smartphone with them at all times

- They believe that most of their clients were more premium brand than own-label, and more current affairs than chat show.

At its core, getting your product or service offering right means answering the question: is what you're selling something that these people want to buy? If it solves a problem they're having, the answer is usually *yes*. Of course, there are also impulse and status purchases. These too will fulfil some basic need, like feeding the ego or wanting a buzz of excitement. However, we're looking at more considered purchases, for which it's likely that the need you're aiming to fulfil will be clearer.

As we saw in chapter three, needs are often a level of abstraction higher than a person might articulate. A manager choosing a document management system for a company, for example, may state that they need version control, audit trails, remote access, etc. But, what they may really *need* is a more productive team. A more productive team might mean that they get more time with their family. Your offering must address both the stated and unstated needs. These normally separate into a pretty emotional and human one, and the specific logical requirements. And, in order of priority, the more human one will win.

WORKED EXAMPLE: VA-VOOM!

The founders spent some time looking back over their notes from past sales meetings. They jotted down the questions they were typically asked. The aim was to work out what requirements were usually on a potential customer's mind when looking for a virtual assistant. At a basic level they agreed that people said that they simply had too much to do and not enough time to do it. When they talked this through, it became clear that the underlying frustration for most was that having so much on their plates was holding them back from doing what they were good at, enjoyed or really wanted to do. A lot of their customers were micro business owners, or high-flying people in larger businesses. When they talked through what these people were like, they found that the common feature was personal ambition. Having lots of, often urgent, administrative tasks to do was stopping them from getting on with the important or strategic work. They agreed on the idea of 'being held back from your true potential' as the real underlying need the VA-Voom! service addressed.

Thinking this way will also open your eyes to the alternative solutions a buyer might have to the same problem. If you only look at organisations that offer similar products and services, you get a distorted view of the options your buyer actually has. For example, using video conferencing might be seen as an alternative to a train journey to see meeting participants in person. Taking the document management requirement again, this might more effectively be addressed with productivity coaching for the team in question, or by recruiting more people. Thinking like this should broaden your ideas about competition. But, more importantly, it should deepen your understanding of how to appeal to the buyer. Getting this right will help you to frame your message in the right language and hook into powerful emotional drivers.

> *If you only look at organisations that offer similar products and services, you get a distorted view of the options your buyer actually has.*

Research the best books on the subjects you come up with and use them as gifts, direct mail, or promotional items.

WORKED EXAMPLE: VA-VOOM!

The VA-Voom! founders really enjoyed this exercise. They'd often looked at other virtual assistant companies, comparing themselves against a direct alternative, but they'd never really thought about how else the need could be met. So, with the emotional need of 'fulfilling your true potential' and the practical need of 'getting stuff done' on their minds they brainstormed all the different ways someone could achieve this.

They came up with:

- Recruiting a part-time or full-time assistant in their own business

- Attending productivity training or workshops

- Working with a personal coach

- Going on a 'personal discovery' retreat

- Investing in various productivity software tools.

For each of these areas they asked one of the assistants to find three examples of companies providing products and services of this kind to review their messaging, pricing, services, etc.

They also asked one of the assistants to spend an hour on Amazon to look for some good books on productivity and personal effectiveness. They were particularly keen on books that had a no-nonsense entrepreneurial feel to them. The following three books looked like they were easily digestible and had the right tone for their clients:

- How to Save an Hour a Day, by Michael Heppell

- Your Best Year Yet!, by Jenny Ditzler

- How to be a Productivity Ninja, by Graham Allcott

Once you've identified a group of people, you can start to really shape what you're selling. Many businesses can articulate their products and services, but still don't have a complete and compelling offering. A product or a service is just one part of your overall proposition.

Go beyond describing your product by asking yourself:

- What are they willing to pay?

- What would they expect for that money?

- How will they know you've delivered on those expectations?

- How quickly would they want you to deliver after purchase?

- How much help and support will they need using the product or service?

- Do you need to see them in person or deal remotely?

- And, crucially, how will their life be tangibly better having bought from you?

Look at competitors and also the products and services that indirectly compete with yours to help assess the market expectations.

When you can answer these questions, you have an offering. This is what marketing folk call a 'proposition'. You need decent answers because, good marketing starts with the truth. Spin, hype or making things look better than they really are is bad, short-term, leaky, marketing. Showing people a genuine solution to a real problem, by providing the tools, time and space in which they make an active choice to use it, is good – Watertight – marketing.

WORKED EXAMPLE: VA-VOOM!

To get a better handle on their full proposition, the VA-Voom! founders spent time looking at current usage and at the various other options available to potential buyers. They also looked at the reasons given by people who either didn't sign up to their service after initial interest, or cancelled their service. In their current client pool there seemed to be a fairly natural split between heavy users, using upwards of 25 hours per month and light users using about 12 hours per month. People who didn't sign up or those who cancelled usually needed a little less than the current monthly minimum. There were also some concerns expressed about being charged for time that wasn't used, and in needing some flexibility to increase hours as and when they were needed. They proposed a three-level service for monthly contracts:

Services	Basic £99 per month	Standard £350 per month	Premium £1,000 per month
Dedicated VA support (9am to 5pm)	2.5 hours	10 hours	30 hours
Out of hours VA support (5pm to 9am)	£50 per hour	£45 per hour	£40 per hour
Additional hours: *If you use more than your monthly allocations, additional hours will be charged at...*	£42 per hour	£40 per hour	£38 per hour
Rollover: *Any unused time will roll over for...*	one month	two months	three months

In your workbook

- Why-why-why

- Your real competitors

- Your proposition

Leak #1 – Forgotten customers

Your customer service – are you available to help?

The ongoing service you provide is part of what your customers pay for. Businesses often think of customer support being triggered by a complaint or service issue of some kind. Even if your service never experiences a problem, customers will think of new questions, their needs might change, a seasonal event might prompt a requirement, a new person might join their team... all sorts of things might happen that mean that they need a little help in using your products or service. And of course... maybe, just maybe, you might make a mistake or let them down in some way.

Where possible, you need to predict what and when service requirements might arise. If you think systematically about how your customers actually use your products and services, you can anticipate their needs and be prepared and proactive about giving them helpful answers to the questions you know will arise. Remember, in this connected world, an unanswered question is an opportunity for a competitor to drill a hole in the side of your Bucket!

Add an FAQs section to your website where you answer everything you usually get asked, and more. There are dynamic plug-ins available to help you manage this from software providers like RightNow and GetSatisfaction.

WORKED EXAMPLE: VA-VOOM!

Each assistant was given a simple twelve-month calendar view on a sheet of A3 paper and asked to jot down any key things that happen every year that might add to their clients' workloads. From this, they were able to create a set of useful blog posts and triggered emails, in which there were sign-posts to buy a few extra top-up hours to deal with:

- Organising the company Christmas party and greetings card

- Getting the bits and pieces they need for their tax return together

- Planning their holidays and dealing with any enquiries whilst they're away

- Setting up out-of-office notices, etc. around public holidays.

They then asked a selection of their best clients to track their working weeks for a month. From this, it became obvious that a great many VA-Voom! clients were working at evenings and weekend. They also asked the web team to look at when to-do items were being added to the system. This verified that out-of-hours was actually a pretty busy time for their clients. This sparked an idea for an additional revenue stream where clients had access to out-of-hours support, at a slightly higher rate. They drew up a one-page description of the service and sent it out to a few clients for feedback. From this they were able to see that there was demand and set a price. To service this they offered their assistants the opportunity to work additional hours at an increased overtime rate. They came up with a rota system where they had one assistant on-call 24-7 and trialled it for six months. This became its own revenue stream and an important service differentiator.

They also added an FAQ area to their website. This quickly proved to be a highly visited area of the site, and is still well-used as links in follow-up emails or in answer to support enquiries. It also had a knock-on benefit to site visits too as the pages started and continue to rank well in natural search results.

It's worth remembering that not everyone will tell you when you've let them down. And, not every need can be anticipated. They may just grumble to themselves, vent angrily in public, or simply cancel their service with you. You need to be proactive. Find ways to identify customers who may be less than satisfied and do something about it:

It's worth remembering that not everyone will tell you when you've let them down.

- Satisfaction tracking

- Mystery calling

- Regular check-ins with their account manager

- Exit interviews or questionnaires with any customers who leave

- Track any indications that usage is tailing off

- Track how much use people are making of the whole service – prompt them if they're missing out.

 Track what your customers are using and highlight any features or benefits they're not making the most of or suggest ways to get even more from what they have.

CASE STUDY: Gradwell

Gradwell, small business Internet service provider and Voice Over Internet specialist, made customer service and satisfaction a key strategic focus three years ago. In that time they've seen a 25 % uplift in overall customer satisfaction. They've worked hard to test and learn what really makes a difference. In addition to introducing helpful guides, webinars, tutorials and online FAQs, they increased their technical support team to keep pace with their growing customer numbers. This ensures that phones are answered quickly and that when people call they get straight through to someone technically competent. They also track their performance carefully with triggered service rating emails and exit interviews with customers who defect. Any incident that's rated below a certain level triggers a personal call from one of the senior technical support team to really understand what happened. One of the key learnings was simply to focus on making the service excellent. Looking into their satisfaction ratings, the politeness and willingness to help of their telephone team always scored highly, but if there was an underlying technical issue, satisfaction was affected. To address this, they recruited a dedicated Service Delivery Manager whose whole focus is to keep the service ticking over, reducing any reasons to call in the first place.

When it comes to customer service, there's a sliding scale in terms of how much it costs your business which is linked to how your customers get in touch. A person finding an article for themselves online is the cheapest; an email or online response within a given timeframe adds a little; picking up the phone for immediate assistance adds more; and seeing someone in person adds significant further costs. So, you need to have a think about who you service in which way. Many well-run businesses will make different service levels available according to the value or importance of the customer in question. Even if you don't differentiate who receives what contact, having an escalation system can work really well for most businesses.

Many well-run businesses will make different service levels available according to the value or importance of the customer in question.

The typical levels of service available, from cheapest to most expensive are:

- Search an online set of help articles and videos

- Send an email that will be answered within 24 hours

- Use an online live chat service

- Speak to a first-line advisor on the telephone

- Speak to a second-line advisor (more expertise) on the telephone

- Allow remote access to your services for an advisor to configure on your behalf

- Arrange a site visit of some kind.

For most businesses a three-level customer support set-up works well: self-serve, by email and by phone. Some more complex or account-managed businesses also need to add in-person to this.

 Structure a customer service system that directs people to the cheaper service channels first, but escalates quickly if they need to.

CASE STUDY: Connect Assist

Connect Assist provides online and telephony support services for charities and social enterprises. Many of these are helpline services where people are looking for timely advice on sensitive matters. One of their clients has been able to extend the reach of their services from roughly 20,000 incidents per year to over 200,000 per year over an 8-year period, whilst reducing the cost per interaction from just under £25 to nearer £3 in the same timeframe. By giving people access to information in three key ways – a self-serve FAQ system, by email, and over the phone – they've been able to help thousands more people without adding much more cost.

You should definitely consider your public social media profiles as a legitimate channel for customers to raise a customer service issue.

With social media channels giving customers more, and more visible, ways to raise their concerns, it's important to track what's being said about you in these places and deal with them appropriately. You should definitely consider your public social media profiles as a legitimate channel for customers to raise a customer service issue.

CASE STUDY: Gradwell

Gradwell provides Internet technology, so it stands to reason that their customers are heavy social media users. To address this they've made sure that they constantly track any enquiries made via these routes and put them into the customer service ticketing system for proper follow-up. Barrie Millett, Commercial Director, goes on to explain why it's been particularly important to listen to the most vociferous of complainants, "Like any technology company, we have a number of highly technical customers who keep us on our toes. It might be easy to dismiss some of their feedback as extreme, or borderline trolling, but if you take the emotion out of it and just listen to the content of what they're telling you, they almost always have something of value to add. And, for every loud and angry customer there are bound be a number more who felt the same, said nothing, but cancelled their service." Since putting customer satisfaction on their strategic agenda, and not least because of their sensible response to social communication, Gradwell has seen a 90 point positive swing in their Net Promoter Score, which indicates how many of their customers would recommend them to others.

Oh, and if you really have made a mistake, be honest about it. Tell people what happened, why, what you're doing about it, and when it will be sorted. Once you've fixed the issue, drop them a line to let them know what you learned and what measures you're taking to make sure it doesn't happen again. Handled well, your response to a mistake can really show your mettle. And, those great books you thought of earlier will make a perfect gift to apologise for the inconvenience.

WORKED EXAMPLE: VA-VOOM!

The whole aim of working with VA-Voom! is to free up a person's time, so they wanted to keep the satisfaction tracking simple. Without vast sums of money available, they decided to use a free online survey tool to set-up a simple 1 to 5 rating with an open field for more feedback. They added this as a link to this client version of the email newsletter and integrated it into their client log-in area. This is where clients manage their to-do lists, track how much time is being used on their account, buy additional hours, etc. and was specially built for them. It includes a function where clients are asked to tag their to-do items with importance and urgency. They chatted to the development team that built the system, and with a day's time a function was added to email the client a link to the satisfaction rating when an item marked as 'important' is ticked off. They introduced a daily task to review the feedback, and where anything rated at less than 4 out of 5 is flagged so that the client is called by one of the founders to ask how the service could have been better. In addition to this, they added an automated email to all clients every 12 weeks to encourage feedback on the service. They noted in their long-term plan a desire to move to a more integrated and automated system for this.

In your workbook

- Service trigger calendar

- Ways to track satisfaction

Your customer communications – do you stay in touch?

Customer service communications are essential. But, it's not the only time you should be talking to your customers. If you're to stay front of mind, and ensure that people feel positive about your company, you'll need to find ways to be friendly and approachable. This is where those positive emotions that people want to move towards really come into play.

You'll need a marketing database to enable customer communications. It's worth using software that's built for the purpose. Salesforce, Capsule or SugarCRM are some good options.

Knowing how much a customer costs to acquire, it is easy to see that keeping a customer, rather than spending the money on finding, winning and setting-up a new one, is a surefire way of stemming a potential hole in your Bucket. An example of this is mobile phone operator, Orange, in the UK. They give all of their customers access to a free cinema ticket for a friend every week. It costs them much less to do this than it would to find a new customer. Take a look at your customers, once you've covered the initial cost of acquisition, and are covering the ongoing costs to serve, how much of the profit that they generate could you reasonably put back into keeping that customer happy so that they stay with you? It doesn't need to be a financial reward. Just being helpful can do the trick.

Invite customers to subscribe to a monthly email in which you share useful ideas and tips. MailChimp has an excellent tool for this.

It's also worth remembering that your existing customers are exposed to the promotional activity you put out for new customers. It can be very irritating for a customer to think that their money is subsidising your new business drive. In which case, something you do to generate demand at the Taps end of the process can cause you to spring a leak at the Bucket end. To avoid this, make sure that you look at your offers and messages through the eyes of both existing and prospective customers.

> *It can be very irritating for a customer to think that their money is subsidising your new business drive.*

Even if what you're offering has no monetary value, your customers won't appreciate finding out about it accidentally. Be proactive in making sure paying customers are the first to hear about your stuff. For example, if you release a new guide or paper or open registrations for an event, simply penning a separate email for existing customers and sending it the day before you tell the world can make them feel valued. You really don't want activity aimed at new customers to de-stabilise the goodwill, and profit, you've built up with existing ones.

 Use the options in your social media accounts to group your customers onto a list so that you can see their interactions quickly. For example, lists on Twitter, Tags on LinkedIn and Circles on Google+.

In some businesses, an annual or service renewal thank you is appropriate, or even a little something on a person's birthday to recognise and reward their loyalty. Hospitality events are definitely worth considering in businesses where you see your customers face to face, or where the exchange is particularly high value. And, there aren't many businesses that couldn't benefit from some friendly interaction in appropriate social media settings. Remember that if a person has an emotional connection to your business they are less price sensitive, more forgiving of mistakes, and much less likely to change suppliers.

WORKED EXAMPLE: VA-VOOM!

The nature of the service provided by VA-Voom! lends itself to relationship building because clients work closely with their named assistant. What became apparent to the founders on talking this through was that they needed to work harder to make the connection with VA-Voom! not just with the individual.

An easy addition to their activity was to tweak their existing monthly email newsletter to create a slightly different version for clients. Looking at their pen portraits and the list of great books they'd come up with when researching around the subject of 'meeting your true potential' gave them the idea to review a book each month. To add some engagement, they started to add a question relating to the book in their private client-only LinkedIn group each month, giving a copy away to the person with the best answer. This content showed their broader understanding of their clients' needs. It also provided a little added value for being an existing client. Looking at their client pen portraits also highlighted that a number of them were under real pressure to fit everything in around young children, especially in school holidays. All the assistants were tasked with tagging if their clients had school-age children. They then got a couple of the assistants with young children to do some desk research and brainstorm ideas to put together top tips and links for busy working parents. After testing this out on a few clients they knew well and getting great feedback, they put this together into an email and PDF download scheduled in their email system to automatically go to appropriately tagged clients ahead of school holidays. From this useful content they signposted a next step: an option to buy some top-up hours to take some of the strain in these busy periods.

It was important to the founders that each client is treated as an individual. So, they decided to add a number of fields to their client database to capture things like birthdays, wedding anniversaries and children's names and birthdays. They used this to set-up triggered reminders to their assistants a week ahead of these dates. Assistants found this useful to make sure they were sent a card from VA-Voom! (and so that they could ensure their clients didn't end up in the doghouse for forgetting an important gift). Rather than just buy cards off the shelf, they used an illustrator from amongst their client list to get a set of greeting cards designed with subtle VA-Voom! branding that they now use for this purpose. Some assistants were better at getting this data than others, so they added client data completeness to their bonus scheme and included it as part of their appraisal reviews.

To make sure that clients were always the first to know about any new content or offers from VA-Voom! they added a system to make sure that anything that went out publicly went to clients 24 hours earlier.

Being exposed to what you say is one thing. But, of course, your customers don't actually belong to you. They live in the world, they read papers, they watch TV, they visit websites – and they will encounter your competitors. And, what your competitors are saying could make your customers question their relationship with you. They might start to feel like they could get something better, cheaper, more fun, etc. elsewhere. So, you can't assume that once a person (or company) has bought from you, that the job is done.

You have to provide regular reassurance that they've made a great decision in using you, and there really is no reason to go anywhere else. If you've gained their permission to stay in touch by email, a recent award or five-star review detailed on your newsletter can add that reassurance. Or, if you've connected with customers in social media, the content you put out there can act to keep people feeling positive about your business. Even a happy customer might defect to a competitor because they highlight a feature that you also offer, but haven't pointed out. Effectively, you need to keep winning that customer so that they stay a customer. It may sound like running to stand still, but it's cheaper than finding new customers. And, naturally, great customer communications also means that they are likely to be favourable to buying more from you.

> *You have to provide regular reassurance that they've made a great decision in using you, and there really is no reason to go anywhere else.*

Investing in great customer service, and regular customer communications that remind people why they chose you, and keep them feeling positive about you will significantly increase how Watertight your Bucket is.

And, remember in all this that your customers have mouths as well as eyes and ears. What they say about the products and services that they receive from you can have a direct impact on other existing, and prospective, customers.

In your workbook

- Database checklist

- Ways to stay in touch

Leak #2 – Poor on-boarding

Your Welcome Window – do they get what they expected?

Of course, your customers will never experience your ongoing customer service and friendly customer communications if they cancel their order in the first few weeks. This is a critical time period. I call this the Welcome Window.

Having framed a proposition that answers all the questions above, and expressed it well in your sales and marketing materials, your buyer will have established expectations along the way. You need to make absolutely sure that you live up to them. Quickly.

It's said that you only get one chance to make a first impression. In securing new business, Adoption, it's more the case that you only have one chance to live up to expectations. And, that's when they're getting started with you. To help people to make the transition between being a new customer, to being a loyal customer you need to treat their first few days and weeks with you with extra care.

> *In securing new business, Adoption, it's more the case that you only have one chance to live up to expectations.*

Handing over their cash is a beginning, not an end, for your buyer. And, these days with social media connecting people at lightning speed, you can be sure that if your buyers feel let down then the world will know about it. Look up #fail on Twitter if you ever want to see a company getting a public roasting.

Search social media sites regularly for both positive and negative mentions of your company.

Initially, people will be in judgement mode, asking themselves questions along logical bases:

- Cost – *is this good value for money?*

- Speed – *is this good use of my time or did it arrive on time?*

- Quality – *is everything in good order?*

- Functionality – *does it perform the task I wanted it to?*

- Dependability – *can it be relied upon to continue delivering?*

> *If you fall foul of any one of these questions, they'll feel emotionally deflated. It's a broken promise.*

If you fall foul of any one of these questions, they'll feel emotionally deflated. It's a broken promise. There are rational ways in which you can let people down – like malfunctioning products, but it's often the subtleties that leave a bad taste. The rational kind are relatively easy to resolve – especially if it's a one-off error that your customer service remedies quickly.

The subtler, more emotional, disappointments can be a harder bridge to mend and are often more keenly felt as an abuse of trust. Remember those positive emotions, and the promise you made of making their life easier. Think about scenarios in which people might:

- Find the product or service set-up harder than they'd believed it would be

- Find unexpected costs that had been hidden away in the small print

- Find out that one of the features they loved isn't included in the package they bought

- Find that the person who pitched to them isn't working on their account

- Find that the tone or manner with which they're handled has a different feel to it.

You need to ensure that you address and answer the obvious. But, you also need to make sure that the personality and emotional connection built up in the sales journey is continued through into service.

This is often about your people. Are they all behaving similarly? Do they all have similar values when it comes to how they do business? Investing in training and activities that help to bring your whole team together can pay dividends in ensuring that your customers experience a consistent style of interaction.

Make sure that marketing, sales and service staff are given opportunities to have fun together, with joint socials or engaging joint projects. Even better, have them report into one line manager.

Think about what happens, from your customers' perspective, when they hand over their cash:

- Do they need to set up some sort of regular payment?

- Do they need to undertake some sort of technical set-up?

- Do they need log-in details?

- Do they need contact details for key people in your business?

Run a workshop where you map out the set-up process for your customers, from their perspective, and then work out how to make this easier for them.

Seeing things from their side of the desk in those crucial early days after they sign on the dotted line means you can provide helpful tools and resources to make this go smoothly, for example:

- A Welcome Pack with key information

- A set of 'How to' tutorial videos

- Checklists and guides

- A follow-up call or email to answer any questions and see how things are going.

Don't just direct people online; put key information in the pack so that it's to hand when and where they need it. For example, a credit-card-sized card, a mousemat, a smartphone app or something they stick to the side of their screen.

It's worth thinking about something that will make them smile too.

These sorts of on-boarding tools will cover those rational bases. It's worth thinking about something that will make them smile too. Something friendly, and unexpected, that's in line with the character of your business. It could be as simple as a thank you card signed by the team, or as elaborate as a personalised video with their account team singing a welcome ditty.

You're aiming for an understanding of the duration of the Welcome Window for your business, or each of your offerings. Once you know what this is, and what people may need from you in this time, you can prepare structured communications to smooth the transition from customer to loyal customer.

WORKED EXAMPLE: VA-VOOM!

The founders pulled out their sales figures from the previous few years to work out how long their Welcome Window was. Using client cancellation data they found that the vast majority of these happened within the first six weeks of signing up. Clients that got past the six-week mark usually stayed with them for over a year. So, they decided to put together a set of welcome communications to cover this period. They put aside a morning with three of their assistants for a brainstorming session. In a two-hour meeting, armed with sticky notes and coffee, they came up with a long list of ideas. This went out to the rest of the team for further feedback and input. Over the following two weeks they tasked each of the assistants to put together the initial content, and had one of them bring it all together to make sure it was in the same tone, and looked great. They came up with:

- A Welcome Pack sent by email to all clients on the first day of their engagement, which includes:

    - Confirmation of their service package

    - Photograph, biography and contact details of their assistant, their back-up assistant, and the team manager

    - For the personal touch, they added a link to a graphology report on each assistant giving some insight into their personality

    - Links to the most popular blog posts

    - Log-in details for the dictation, to-do lists and account management area

    - Links to how-to videos on using the client log-in area

    - A link to an archive of client newsletters with details of how to amend contact preferences

    - A discount voucher to use against the pre-packaged template products.

- For clients on the middle package, a postal version was created which included a credit-card-sized pack of key contact information and a print-out of one of their most popular posts.

- For clients on the premium package, they made a selection of business books available from which the assistants could choose something appropriate. This was included in the postal pack as a welcome gift with a hand-written card.

- They introduced a system to tag new customers in the email system to receive:

  - A daily productivity tip by email for the first month

  - A weekly how-to guide and video on key activities; for example: Top Tips for Effective Dictation; How to Delegate a Task; Diary Management Tips; Useful things you can do in under 5 minutes.

- A personal call by the team manager at 2 weeks, 4 weeks and 6 weeks.

They made a note in the diary to review this set of materials every six months to make sure it was still up to date and make improvements.

In your workbook

- What's your Welcome Window?

- The let down list

- On-boarding map

- Welcome Pack checklist

- Uncommon courtesy

Leak #3 – No emotional connection

Your brand or reputation – what kind of people are you?

All of the elements above come together to really sum up what your company is about. It's what will determine how it feels to be a customer of yours. It is what builds your company reputation. This happens over time, but there are some foundations you need to lay. And those are what your company looks and sounds like.

 If you've worked hard to make sure it's easy to do business with you, and that your service is helpful and friendly – but what's written on your website is hard to read, and the imagery you've chosen is cold and distant – you're missing a trick. Technology companies are often a prime example of this. They think that they need to make it clear that they do technical things, and use pictures of servers and wires to illustrate this. But, people aren't buying wires, they're buying what the wires help them with. And, remember it's those positive emotions that work most effectively here.

 Go back to those emotional needs you came to using why-why-why and use imagery that relates to them.

Your company's visual identity is built up through things like colour, typography, imagery and layout. A visual identity that expresses the real character of your business, and hooks into the emotional needs that your services fulfil will work harder for you than one that is wholly logically driven.

CASE STUDY: Ascentor

Ascentor, an information risk consultancy, was having trouble differentiating their business. They provide high-value consulting services, where they really understand the client in question and build a holistic information security strategy specifically for them, covering everything from their people policies to IT systems. They found themselves competing against businesses selling off-the-shelf technical quick fixes. Looking at their marketing materials, it was hard to tell Ascentor apart from these types of competitor. Their imagery was almost identical – pictures of computers and data represented in binary code. Working with an experienced team, they developed a new visual identity that more accurately expressed the sense of their big picture approach and enabled Ascentor to move the conversation beyond the server cupboard.

 Prepare a set of visual identity guidelines detailing your company colours, logo usage, fonts, imagery, etc. and make sure all materials are created in the same style.

Take a look at all of your documentation, websites and presentations. You should have a set style for things like headings and sub-headings. Do You Use Leading Capital Letters, or MAYBE YOU CAPITALISE PRIMARY HEADINGS? Then there are lists and numbering. Do you use Roman Numerals, Numerics, and do you present reports with legal numbering throughout? Work this stuff out. Make it consistent.

Invest in a set of Template documents in which these styles are pre-set and train people on how to use them.

CASE STUDY: VPW Systems

 VPW provides a one-stop-shop for small business IT in Devon. They really wanted to set themselves apart as a local provider, with all the friendliness and accessibility that brings, but with the highest possible standards. Having spent some time codifying all the visual elements of the brand, they made an investment in a set of professionally-produced templates for Microsoft Office documents. These are now used to create all of their documentation. Managing Director, Vince Wilton, comments, "We spent a lot of money on the templates upfront, but they are probably the single biggest improvement I've made in our marketing. I now regularly get unsolicited compliments on the quality of our documents." It was important for VPW to demonstrate that they have real attention to detail in everything they do. Having documents that consistently look the part is important to getting this message across.

25 Your visual identity is important in getting people to understand your business. The written and spoken word are also essential, as well as the tone you use. For some reason, people often feel that when it comes to writing something official, like copy for a company website, they need to adopt a formal writing style. But, it can be much more compelling to write in a more 'spoken word' style.

 Think about how you would speak if you were in a room with the people you have in mind; write as if you're actually talking to them.

A starting point for setting your written and spoken style is to address the basics. This means having consistent spelling conventions. For example, is it email, Email or e-mail? If you operate in English, do you use American or British spellings? Is it appropriate in your business to use contractions, like 'isn't' or 'won't' or do your customers expect a more formal tone? You may also wish to provide guidance to people on the use of dashes, colons, etc. so that all of your material has a similar feel to it. If you're a more modern company, it might even be appropriate to allow people to break some rules of grammar. For example, starting sentences with And and But. These things all come together to give a style to your writing, express your personality and give a sense of what it is like to work with you.

> *These things all come together to give a style to your writing, express your personality and give a sense of what it is like to work with you.*

Build up a company manual of spelling conventions, your use of capitalisation, etc. and make sure all your people use it.

Having addressed the basics, it's time to move on to a little of the beauty. This is where the real humanity comes through. I'm less able to be prescriptive here, as it's often more about attitude and tone. An example might be the use of metaphor to express what you do. Perhaps you could build up a set of common analogies and metaphors that people can use... like the Bucket, Funnels and Taps in this book. Is there something that could bring what you do to life? There's also humour. It can be hard to get this one right, but if you do, it works brilliantly. The best way to help your people understand this is to provide examples of what works, and what doesn't. If you ever want an example of a company getting this right, look at email providers MailChimp. Their character shines through and their humour is cheeky without being offensive or flippant.

Prepare tone of voice guidelines to help people understand how your business should sound. Use examples of writing that's right, and copy that's wrong, explaining why.

Then there are your people. It's trite to say that people buy from people; it's been said a thousand times. But, that is because it is true. It can be extremely powerful to bring the individual personalities of the people in your business to the fore. If you're recruiting people into your business who share your values, and you've given them the tools and training to understand your brand, you should trust them to go public. Account handlers and senior people on your team really should be engaging in social media as themselves and writing blog posts under their own name. You can also bring a little personality by:

> *Account handlers and senior people on your team really should be engaging in social media as themselves and writing blog posts under their own name.*

- Having unusual profile photography taken that says something about them

- Adding an interesting or unusual question to their standard professional biography

- Showing their photo as part of their byline on blog posts or newsletter contributions.

 Get professional photos taken of your key people in a company style, so that there's some consistency, and you're showing your faces.

CASE STUDY: VPW Systems

VPW wanted to show some personality, but the team was a bit uncomfortable with being featured in the marketing, and they had struggled to find cost-effective stock photography that actually looked like their own people or their clients. Managing Director, Vince Wilton, comments, "We operate in Exeter, and whilst the small businesses around here are extremely professional, they're certainly not all suited and booted. The ubiquitous 'smiley-office-worker-in-a-suit' stock shots look nothing like us or the people we actually deal with". To give a human touch to their brand, they went for a set of three hand-drawn characters, each with their own scenario that a typical VPW client could really empathise with. These now form the central theme that runs through their website and marketing materials. Vince continues, "I love our characters, Bob, Mary and Dan, they really help me to explain what we do, and they make us look completely different from any other IT support company around here."

WORKED EXAMPLE: VA-VOOM!

The emotional connection that VA-Voom! wanted to make with their customers and prospective customers was one of taking some of the burden from them. Specifically, they wanted to hook into the feelings of stress and frustration that come from not being able to do your best at something because you have too much on your plate. For their high-flying audience this often meant never quite making time to work on those things that really take them forwards. VA-Voom! wanted to show their service as the answer to this. They wanted to give people the sense that working with VA-Voom! would give them back the time they need to meet their true potential.

They printed out a copy of 'How to write a marketing brief' from the Watertight Marketing website and used it to pull their information together. They then used this to brief a local branding agency and worked with them to produce a full Style Guide for their visual and written identity (you can download a full copy of this from watertightmarketing.com). Because working with a named assistant was core to the service, VA-Voom! decided to make its people central. They invested in professional photography that featured their people, including profile photos that expressed a little of their individual character.

They then did an audit of all their materials and allocated a 12-week window to bring everything in line with the new identity. The two key investments off the back of this was the website and a set of Microsoft templates. They also made sure that all of the assistants were fully trained on the new brand and using the templates, and included it as part of their induction process for any new joiners.

To make sure that the personalities of the assistants came through enough to make the VA-Voom! style really human, but without making them uncomfortable, they held a working session with the team. They decided to:

- Set up Twitter identities for each individual but with VA-Voom! in the name, e.g. @VAVoomSarah. They agreed some guidelines on how these would be used.

- Have a graphology report undertaken on each assistant and published an adapted version of it on their web profiles. This was a bit of fun, added some personality and showed the individuality of their team.

- Add an 'about the author' block at the bottom on each blog post that features the photograph of the author, their social media links and a link to their personal profile. On their profile, links to their top posts are now displayed.

- Invest in some social media training for the whole team to encourage them to engage comfortably and professionally. They decided to budget to refresh this training quarterly to keep up with new techniques and to bring new joiners up to speed.

In your workbook

- Visual identity checklist

- Tone of voice checklist

- Can you template it?

- Photography checklist

- Show some personality

If you're able to answer the five questions laid out in this chapter then you will have something in place for each of the core marketing tasks for this stage. Here you're looking to **be friendly** and **be consistent**. If you're meeting these tasks, you'll have stemmed the first three leaks that mean that the time, energy and money that you spend in filling your Bucket is not wasted.

Your Watertight Bucket Checklist

Step	Leak	Think about
ADOPTION BE FRIENDLY	**3** NO EMOTIONAL CONNECTION	*What kind of people are you?* Visual identity • Tone of voice • The personal touch
	2 POOR ON-BOARDING	*Do they get what they expected?* • Welcome Window • Welcome Pack • New customer communications
LOYALTY BE CONSISTENT	**1** FORGOTTEN CUSTOMERS	*Do you stay in touch?* • Customer communications *Are you available to help?* • Three-level customer support • Customer satisfaction tracking • Proactive service communication

Further reading:

- **Bly, R. W. (2005) 2nd ed.** *Copywriter's Handbook: A Step-by-Step Guide to Writing Copy That Sells,* **Henry Holt & Co**

- **Bounds, A. (2007)** *The Jelly Effect: How to Make Your Communication Stick,* **Capstone Press**

- **Daffy, C. (1999) 2nd ed.** *Once a Customer Always a Customer,* **Oak Tree Press**

- **Maslen, A. (2007)** *Write to Sell: The Ultimate Guide to Great Copywriting,* **Marshall Cavendish**

- **McDonald, M. and Rogers, B. (2001)** *Key Account Management,* **Butterworth Heinmann**

- **Townsend, H. (2011)** *FT Guide to Business Networking: How to Use the Power of Online and Offline Networking for Business Success,* **Pearson**

Your Funnels, not funnel

If all of your customers come from just one source, you're either missing a trick or you're on dangerous ground. The most successful businesses have identified a number of different ways of getting themselves noticed. This is not least because different people respond to different things, but also to reduce the chances of someone turning off a single Tap, and with it your income. This means you'll also need a number of Funnels to channel new customers to your Bucket.

Having shored up your Bucket, it can be tempting to turn the Taps on. But, before you do so you'll need to make sure you have appropriate Funnels in place. Here we're looking to get people through the **Evaluation** and **Trial** stages of their buying decision. To do this, we're plugging a further three leaks by answering these five key questions:

Leak #4 – No gateway – An effective way of allowing people to try what you have on offer before making a significant commitment. To do this, you should consider:

- Product ladder – *is there a tiered path into payment?*

- Enabling trial – *can people try without commitment?*

Leak #5 – No critical approval – Understanding who your buyer turns to before deciding to buy and ensuring that those people are on your side. At this stage you're addressing:

- Decision makers – *who can say no?*

Leak #6 – No proof – Backing up every promise you make with appropriate evidence and factual information. Powerful sources of logical proof include:

- Third party endorsement – *what are people saying about you?*

- Facts and figures – *where's the evidence?*

When these things are brought together, your business will be able to survive even the toughest of scrutiny.

Surviving scrutiny

One of the biggest barriers to long-term profits can be rushing your potential buyer into parting with their cash before they've really got a sense of what it would be like as one of your customers. In the middle part of the process, you'll need to set out your stall to let your buyers scrutinise what's really on offer. Giving your buyers space to evaluate your offering, and finding innovative ways of enabling them to Trial your products and services, will increase your ultimate customer value and your chances of establishing long-term relationships. It may mean learning to be happy to let some people walk away. This will be either because you have the integrity to admit that their needs are not best met by you, or the confidence to know that your business needs are not best met by them.

> *It may mean learning to be happy to let some people walk away.*

Leak #4 – No gateway

Product ladder – is there a tiered path into payment?

For many businesses, the key obstacle to this steadier sales approach is not having a decent product ladder – that is, a complementary set of products or services that lead from an initial lower value, or lower risk, purchase through to a premium one. Equipping your sales team, or website, with a compelling first purchase to which your buyer can easily say *yes*, can have a really powerful effect. Especially if you have this linked to appropriate 'next steps'.

A robust product ladder might look something like this:

	Knowledge business e.g. Marketing Consultancy	Product business e.g. Men's grooming	Online tool e.g. Accountancy software
Gateway Offer	Free Online Tool *Online Mini Audit*	Free Sample *Disposable Razor Blade*	Free Version *Two-week Trial*
Gateway Product	Paid Audit & Report *3-day Marketing Audit*	Core product *Razor Blade*	Basic Version *Single User*
Real Profits!	Consulting Exercise *12-month Transformation Programme*	Matching set *Shaving Foam, Moisturiser, etc.*	Premium Version *Multi-user*
On to...	Ongoing Support *Outsourced Marketing Management*	Ongoing... *Replenishments*	Add-ons *Credit Control Letter Templates, etc.*

Some businesses will have fewer rungs on their product ladder than these examples. For some, there's merit in making this an uncomplicated two-step ladder. Just the free trial, and then a simple one-price option. This works particularly well for subscription models, where there's just one low monthly fee for which you get everything you need. More complex businesses, like those offering bespoke systems build and servicing, may need to provide additional rungs to include such things as 'proof of concept' and contractual break clauses.

Whatever the business model, the chief concern is making their first purchase as risk free as possible. This allows the buyer to genuinely assess your business before committing to a vast spend or ongoing engagement. It gives you the opportunity to really show what you're made of. This is where a Gateway Product that is self-contained and useful in its own right can work brilliantly. Don't just re-package a sales visit into something they pay for. If you are asking someone to part with their cash, you need to give them something of value in return. Remember the fundamental marketing task at this stage is to be helpful.

In knowledge-based or consultancy businesses, a product ladder isn't just about letting them get to you know, it also means that you can get to know them. This is really powerful. The combination of gaining their trust through a well-delivered Gateway Product or project, and building up a good understanding of their needs, allows you to put a meatier proposal to them for the next sale. This translates into a higher eventual spend and greater ongoing commitment than they would have made if the Gateway hadn't been available. The opposite is also true. Sometimes the initial engagement will also alert you to the fact that they're not a great fit for your business, and you can walk away before you've put hours into kicking off a long-term relationship.

Pricing is paramount in designing an effective Gateway Product. You need to know how much your buyer can authorise without having to involve other people. This is the perfect price point. It means they can buy and try your services under their own steam, and then later go to their Board, wife, or other joint decision maker with a suggestion to step up to the next level. It needs to be priced low enough to be a minimal financial risk, but high enough that they'll value the output.

> *You need to know how much your buyer can authorise without having to involve other people. This is the perfect price point.*

A price that everyone can afford is free. This is where a Gateway Offer comes into play. Including a completely free first step can have a dramatic effect on uptake. Smartphone applications are a great example of this, where a free version is often made available to give you a flavour of the full paid-for version. The upgrade path, and communications to facilitate this, needs to be really compelling. It is worth noting that in some markets, free can signal 'of no value'. This is where online tools and calculators can be useful, because they capture a little of your expertise without giving valuable time away for free.

Can you create an online tool or calculator that gives people an experience of your business before they move onto a paid engagement?

CASE STUDY: Ascentor

> Information risk consultancy, Ascentor, offers holistic information security expertise to businesses and governmental organisations. This covers everything from technical reviews to people and policies. On their website you can take a free 12-question 'Risk Review' that gives an indication as to how much information risk your business is currently exposed to. This leads into a nurtured sales approach, in which the Gateway Product is a fixed-price information security audit.

Product-based businesses often struggle with the concept of a Gateway Offer, as it's often perceived that people either buy the product, or they don't. Free samples work well, but can be a prohibitive upfront expense. If you think creatively, there's often an interesting way to get people to start engaging with your offer without an expensive outlay. Smartphone apps, online tools, calculators and games can do the job nicely.

CASE STUDY: Fable Trading

Fable Trading, the UK & Ireland distributors of Trollbeads charm bead jewellery, implemented an effective product ladder for their highly tangible product range. The concept is that the customer buys a range of interchangeable items with which they create their own bracelets, necklaces and earrings. The core product is a bracelet, with a lock and a selection of beads. The Gateway Offer is a free online Wish List, where people can browse and save lists of the jewellery they desire. Setting up a Wish List also acts as a mechanism for securing email marketing permission. The Gateway Product is a Debut Bracelet, which is effectively a 'starter kit' including a chain, a lock and two beads. Once a customer has their bracelet, they are invited into ongoing communications to continue building their collection. These communications include newsletters, competitions, social media interaction and in-store events. This encourages loyalty and ongoing bead purchases. The add-ons in this product ladder are extending their collection with the necklaces and earrings.

Another essential ingredient is how much commitment you're asking for. Many businesses use a free trial as some sort of honey trap, where cancelling the service is difficult. For a Gateway to be at its most effective, I firmly believe that there should be no structural lock-in or hefty commitment on the part of the customer. The whole point is to make the buying decision easy. If you put in loads of caveats and tie-ins, you're adding complication… which means added thinking time and reasons to say no. Make it a simple purchase with no further obligation. It's then the job of your sales and marketing (and of course the quality of your product and customer service) to turn this into a loyal customer. This goes back to having confidence in your offering. If it genuinely meets their needs, and you can show this, then they should go on to buy. If it doesn't, them not buying from you is almost certainly the right decision for you both.

Remove anything from your Gateway Offer that means the buyer needs to ask the opinion of others.

Timing is also critical in a product ladder. Don't leave it too long between one step and the next. Your Gateway Offer, for example, needs to be long enough to allow people to make an initial assessment, but not so long as it slips off their radar.

Test the length of your trial period to ensure that trialists actually engage with your offer in that time.

CASE STUDY: KashFlow

KashFlow offers a completely free trial of their software. The buyer signs no contract, hands over no money and no credit card details. Their Chief Executive, Duane Jackson, explains, "It's about reducing all the barriers and making it as simple as it can possibly be to try the service. Then it's about confidence in what you have to offer. You shouldn't need a lock-in if what they're trying does what you said it will." And, it works, the majority of people who take up their free trial convert into paying customers. Duane continues, "When we changed our free trial from two months to two weeks, conversions went up by 25 %. It meant that buyers actually looked at the software in that time window, rather than thinking they had long enough to look at it later but never quite getting around to it."

Having a clear product ladder, with each rung providing something of genuine value, is a gift to any decent salesperson. It always means there's something tangible to talk about and useful to provide, without a hefty price tag or commitment.

WORKED EXAMPLE: VA-VOOM!

The VA-Voom! team found it hard to come up with a Product Ladder as they couldn't initially see how to give people a way into the service without giving time away for free. They were concerned that this would devalue their service and, as it can take a little while for the client to get really good at delegating, if a trial was too short they thought it might be counter-productive.

Taking the advice to give people what they need to be helpful to their buying decision, they decided to look at the questions they typically get asked. The one that came up consistently was 'How much time could I save?' So, they designed a questionnaire to help people work out for themselves how much time could be saved by working with a virtual assistant. They called it the *Time Saver Analyser* and it became the first step on their ladder, a free Gateway Offer. With a little investment with their web team, prospects are now presented with a list of typical tasks, they input how much time they estimate they spend on each task. They're then asked to rate how easy that task would be to delegate. They're also asked their annual earnings, how many hours a week they typically work, and how many hours they'd like to work. This information is used to produce a personalised report of how much time per year a Virtual Assistant is likely to save them, and roughly how much this would be worth. To hook into the really strong positive emotions and add some proof to these reports they collated examples of what other clients had achieved in similar amounts of time. These included things like: writing a book, planning a new business, studying for a degree, climbing Everest, attending a singing workshop and attending a weekly exercise class. The assistants were able to select from amongst these when putting a personalised report together to give a sense of what the prospect might do in the time that would be freed up.

They decided to make the next step on their ladder a paid trial, in which a full *Time Saver Audit* was undertaken. They felt that one month was the shortest period in which it was possible to see whether a VA relationship would work. In this month, clients are given a worksheet to complete that tracks exactly what they were doing with their time, and at the end of each week they have a call with their assistant to review it and see if any of the tasks could have been handed off. At the end of the month, the assistant they've been working with presents the findings of the Audit with suggestions for more effective use of time and a suggested working relationship with VA-Voom! To make this trial even more compelling, they decided to underwrite it with a satisfaction guarantee. This created a stepping stone to the contracted relationship, from which there is an up-sell to a greater package and top-up hours. Templates and events could then be sold as appropriate. The Product Ladder they came up with looks like this:

Step	Offer	Details
Gateway Offer	Time Saver Analyser	Free online tool to give an indication of how much time could be saved and the financial value of that.
Gateway Product	Time Saver Audit	£350 for 10 hours support over one month and a full Time Saver Audit with money-back guarantee.
Ongoing Relationship	Three-Level Package	One of the three packages ranging from £99 to £1,000 per month, with a 3-month notice period.
Up-sell	Top-up hours	At the rate within their package.
Cross Sell	VA-Voom! Events and Templates	Conferences and skills sessions. Key documents and training.

Enabling trial – can people try without commitment?

If you've added a free trial to your product ladder, you'll be forgiven for thinking that you have this one covered, but there's a distinction to be made between low commitment and no commitment.

If you're asking for their data, that can be a step too far. With email and telephone marketing tainted by spammers, people are often reticent to try something that looks like an invitation for a salesperson to get in touch. This can seem pushy. Adding in a softer way of giving a potential buyer a feeling for being your customer can reap significant rewards.

> *You need to provide a window on your business through which people can peer unencumbered.*

You need to provide a window on your business through which people can peer unencumbered. It's the equivalent of letting people browse in a shop. By all means, say hello and let them know where you are if they need you, but give them space to look around.

For complete freedom to look at your company without any fear of being hassled, make the following available without any sign-up forms or requests for data:

- Open-to-all webcasts and tutorials

- Video tours and interviews

- Papers and articles

- Product demonstrations or visualisations.

To draw people in further, but with a light touch, think about:

- Expert Q&A sessions where people ask questions via social media

- Live web or telephone seminars for which people register

- In-person seminars or workshops.

CASE STUDY: Fable Trading

Helping customers to realise the creative potential of owning a wide range of interchangeable Trollbeads jewellery components is essential to getting people engaged with the product. To bring this to life the UK & Ireland distributors, Fable Trading, use a proportion of their visual merchandiser's time to engage in social media activity. Each week she puts together a seasonal or themed set of jewellery, which is photographed and shared on their Facebook page. And, on a monthly basis she hosts a live Q&A session via Facebook and Twitter where customers can ask her advice. Questions have ranged from ideas for beads to suit a wedding theme, to how to convince a partner to buy Trollbeads jewellery as a gift.

The aim here is to give a sense of what it would be like to be your customer. This serves two purposes. It helps people to see if you can do what you say you can, and it also gives them a sense of what it would feel like to be a customer of yours. It's about *showing* people what you do, not telling them. And, by showing them, I don't mean showing off. I mean being genuinely helpful.

Set aside about 10% of your top experts' time for participating in these sorts of activities. Think about working it into their job role and appraisals.

WORKED EXAMPLE: VA-VOOM!

The question for the VA-Voom! team was: 'How can we show people what we do without actually working as their assistant?' It was again time for brainstorming with a handful of assistants. They were looking for two sorts of activity: something really grounded and practical, and something that hooked into the positive emotions of meeting your potential. The first idea was devastatingly simple. Each assistant was asked to think of 10 ways to save five minutes. They picked the best ideas from these and set up a decent video camera in the lightest of their meeting rooms. With a small investment in some desktop video editing software and some stock soundtracks, they turned out a series of video snippets using these tips. They set up a YouTube channel and scheduled to upload one new tip each month. Using the 'embed' clip button on YouTube they were also able to put these videos on their own website in a section called 'Time Saver Tips'. This met the need to give people a really practical example of what they do, it was useful in and of itself, and showed a bit of personality. What it didn't do was hook into the real human driver of meeting your potential. One of the founders was a pretty good public speaker and had done a few talks at local networking groups. So, she looked back over her presentation material. One of them sparked an idea which they worked up into a monthly web seminar, entitled *'Making Time to Meet Your Potential'*. To give it some extra credibility they invited a respected personal effectiveness coach who was one of their clients to become a co-presenter of the session. They came up with 10 key barriers to meeting your potential, and for each they mapped out three ideas for overcoming them. So, in the one-hour session people are given 30 actionable ideas. Just one of these is to work with a virtual assistant.

In your workbook

- Product ladder checklist
- Gateway offers
- A no-commitment trial
- Gateway pricing checklist

Leak #5 – No critical approval

Decision makers: who can say no?

As we saw in chapter five, third parties aren't just an influence, sometimes they can make or break a sale. It's usually at about this point in the process where people who must be consulted come into the frame. If they're not on your side, you have yourself a leak. You can overcome this by communicating with that person directly, or by equipping your buyer to do the convincing for you. Ideally, both.

In the corporate world, for example, you'll find companies selling services to a buyer in a given discipline like human resources or marketing, running campaigns that target the financial director. For really large purchases, or for strategic investments, you may need to address the needs of the whole Board. This is known in marketing circles as the Decision Making Unit. This phenomenon isn't confined to the business world. Families are often a Decision Making Unit. In consumer electronics there's a beautifully politically-incorrect term used for this – it's the 'wife-approval factor'.

CASE STUDY: Ascentor

Dave James, from information risk consultants Ascentor, comments, "Securing a company's information covers every part of the organisation. The responsibility often lies with IT, but a firewall will never stop a person letting important information slip on an overheard phone call, or a filing cabinet being left unlocked." Recognising that IT teams needed to educate their peers, they prepared 'The Board's Guide to Information Risk'. This equipped them to have the wider and more strategic conversation. This was bolstered with a research-driven public relations campaign that demonstrated how information security is a company-wide issue. Dave continues, "This meant that when our buyer brought the subject up internally, it was likely that their colleagues had already been exposed to the idea, and our company name. For us, this meant sales conversations were more holistic which ultimately led to more wide-ranging, and profitable, engagements."

What's crucial, in a considered purchase, is that there are often third parties with more than just influence. There are people you may never talk to with a power of veto. You need to know who they are, and you need to get them on-side. You can do this by preparing materials specifically for them, or make some tools available that your buyer uses to do the sales job for you. Another really powerful technique is to partner with a complementary organisation that already has the ear of the person in question. For example, a human resources company might put on a free seminar for the existing clients of a local law firm.

 In business-to-business markets, look at any key prospects' company pages on LinkedIn to see if their colleagues are listed.

WORKED EXAMPLE: VA-VOOM!

For personal contracts, they found that the decision was usually made by the person in question. In larger organisations this was often signed off by human resources and finance. And, even where the decision was made by an individual, they still asked themselves these logical questions. The VA-Voom! founders had worked on objection responses to using a virtual assistant a number of times over the years. They hadn't thought of bringing them together into a piece of marketing content. Working as a pair, with flipchart and pen, they mapped out a paper which they called 'The Real Cost of Self-Administration'. They took three angles: financial, productivity and potential. In the working session they bullet-pointed what they wanted to say. They then worked on it over a fortnight in evening and weekends until they had a 2000-word paper, which they made available on their website in return for subscribing to their monthly newsletter. To allow people some access to the material without providing their data, they produced three presentations summarising each of the three sections for which they recorded a voiceover and placed as videos on their YouTune channel. They also adapted versions of the material as blog posts. To make the material go even further, and to make sure it got in front of key decision makers, they also tailored a number of the posts for a reader from each of the influencing disciplines and offered them as guest posts on websites aimed at these people. The presentations and posts all pointed back to the download. They also had a number nicely printed and bound at a local print shop to use in sales meetings and as follow-up to inbound enquiries.

In your workbook

- Who can say no?

Leak #6 – No proof

Before someone puts their neck out to recommend your company to a colleague or spouse, or before they spend precious time trying your services out, they'll need to believe that you can indeed solve their problem. This is about trusting that you can deliver what you say you can. Amongst many others, there are two guaranteed ways that you can build this trust. The first is through the power of third parties, and the second is with evidence.

> *This is about trusting that you can deliver what you say you can.*

Third party endorsement – what are people saying about you?

If a salesperson tells you that his product is amazing, you'll be forgiven for suspending disbelief. If someone you already trust tells you they're amazing, you're likely to listen.

The first place to start is with your existing customers, because it's great to have customers who are quietly happy with what you do, but it's even better to have customers who are loudly happy about what you do. There are three ways to encourage existing customers to support your business:

1. Make it easy for them to pass information on.

2. Get them to publicly endorse your business.

3. Reward them for the referrals they make.

You will find that happy customers will naturally tell other people about you. In my consulting business, we do this all the time with the various marketing tools and systems we use. If something works, we love telling people about it – particularly clients – because knowing these things is part of the value we bring. If what you're doing is good quality, then this will happen without your input, but it will happen even more with a little nurturing from you. If you make it easy for people to spread the word, then they are more likely to do so. This has been made increasingly simple, with many free ways to add one-click buttons to your emails and web pages that let people email it to others or share it in social media.

> *If you make it easy for people to spread the word, then they are more likely to do so.*

 Add a 'share' or 'forward' option to your web pages and marketing emails.

Public endorsements are also easier than ever to get these days. With social media sites, such as LinkedIn, providing tools for people to leave feedback on people and products they've used. There's nothing to stop you generating great third party endorsements for what you do. Don't leave this to chance. Build collecting endorsements into your business processes. If you have a formal satisfaction programme, people who score you above a certain level could be asked to leave an endorsement. For smaller businesses, or where you have a more direct relationship with customers, simply adding a note to a project wrap-up checklist to ask for an endorsement can generate some excellent feedback that's in the public domain. Depending on the nature of your business, you could also build a review system into your website. For a knowledge-based business or one with a small product set, the endorsements on the product listing of LinkedIn company pages work well. For those with larger product ranges a star-rating system can be effective.

> *Don't leave this to chance. Build collecting endorsements into your business processes.*

 Add a link in your customer communications to where customers can leave a public review or endorsement.

WORKED EXAMPLE: VA-VOOM!

The VA-Voom! website had a few client testimonials already, but they weren't named and you couldn't tell what level of service the clients were talking about. Having settled on their three packages they went through their client database to find existing clients on these payment levels. Each assistant was then asked to call their clients if they felt it was appropriate to ask if they'd be happy to appear in a case study video. Working with a professional videographer, they invested in two case study videos for each level of service – six in total. They decided to put a line in the budget to add three new videos every six months. They chose clients to approach by tracking the satisfaction ratings. They continue to use these to generate online testimonials. Clients who rate the service as 5/5 are approached for testimonials directly. They are sent an email thanking them for their feedback in which there's a link and details on how to leave a public recommendation for the service on the VA-Voom! LinkedIn page. They continue to use these testimonials around their website, on their sales materials, in their Welcome Pack and email newsletters. Assistants were also encouraged to ask for personal testimonials on their own LinkedIn profile, which are then re-used on their company profiles too.

CASE STUDY: KashFlow

Those clever people at KashFlow wanted to make powerful use of the high number of totally unsolicited, and brilliant, customer comments that were coming to them via Twitter. So, they got their software people to create a little tool that live feeds any positive mentions of the company on Twitter onto their website homepage.

You can also reward this behaviour with what's called affiliate or referral marketing. This is where you pay people for the prospective customers they send your way. You can do this manually, by publishing a simple referral policy, or in an automated way setting up an affiliate scheme online. These schemes allow you to set up ads people can use on their own websites, and web links with unique identifiers that automatically keep a tally of the various things that you might pay people for, from a small amount for traffic they generate, to a larger cut on actual paying business that came via them. You'll typically find that leads that come through a referral are much cheaper to generate in the first place, and will also often result in a quicker and higher value sale because the new customer trusts the opinion of the person who pointed them in your direction. If you feel uncomfortable paying people for their referrals, or perhaps if it sits awkwardly with your or their values, most affiliate schemes now give the option for people to donate any earnings to a charity.

 Think about how much a referred lead is worth to you. Offer some of that back to the referrer, either in monetary form or as a discount on purchases.

WORKED EXAMPLE: VA-VOOM!

The easiest thing the VA-Voom! team did to encourage people to pass their material on was to get the web team to add a 'share this' button throughout their website. This was a half-hour job and started getting their content out there immediately. They also asked one of the team to research affiliate marketing. She found a way to make their *Time Saver Tips* go even further. Each time they issue a new video, they make it available on Coull. This lets productivity bloggers and site owners use the VA-Voom! video tips on their sites with a button on the video player that links back to the paper 'The Real Cost of Self-Administration'. They pay the site owners a small fee for everyone who clicks through. They also came up with a really simple referral scheme, which they manage manually. It pays out 2.5 % of the three-month income of any new client to the person who referred them. There's also an option for this money to be paid to a charity of their choice. The scheme is promoted to all existing clients and to complementary businesses with whom they have a good relationship. They also got some digital business cards printed with the basic details of this which they always have to hand for networking breakfasts and the like.

So, nurturing your existing customers can generate you more business, more cheaply. They're also extremely valuable should there ever be a negative opinion to counter. When people are making that crucial final buying decision, other people can put them off. For example, they could read a bad review. Businesses who've really given excellent service and nurtured their customers, will find that these people become a defence against criticism. It is so much more powerful to have a customer refute a bad review than someone from your company. And if you've been active in building relationships, in social media in particular, then you'll have an army of web-savvy people at hand to rally around if an occasion arises for them to do so.

Give customers somewhere to easily feed back the good and the bad; it makes it far less likely that they will vent angrily in public.

Of course, it's not just customers who can influence your buyers. Think about their wider circle too. Nurturing relationships with people who work with the same types of people as you in a complementary or non-competitive way is well worth your effort. For example, an accountant and a law firm offering services to small businesses would make an excellent co-referring relationship for a business providing outsourced human resource management. All these people keep the market talking. The blog articles, how-to guides, etc. that you're writing are often perfect materials for third parties to point others to if asked for a recommendation.

Facilitating situations in which interesting people can have interesting conversations, about anything – not just business – is often the best way of generating high quality referrals.

If you have a large database, you can be really smart about this. Many systems allow you to review influence scoring systems, like Klout or PeerIndex, to show you who in your subscriber or customer list is particularly influential. You could use this to tailor the material they receive.

It's also worth remembering that from conversations come sales. Facilitating situations in which interesting people can have interesting conversations, about anything – not just business – is often the best way of generating high quality referrals.

Identify your key referrers and ensure that you've invited them to receive updates of your new content.

CASE STUDY: Ovation Finance

Referrals are one of Ovation Finance's most important sources of new business. To help this along, they host a monthly social event. They have an interesting speaker on a topic that's outside of business. The aim is simply to have interesting conversations. There are no targets to meet. No elevator pitches delivered. Chris Budd, Managing Director, comments, "It's amazing how much business gets done when you tell people that the event is not about business. It seems to take the pressure off somehow and people just get chatting."

There's also the media, and social media, in your sector to think about here. You will want your buyers to hear good things about you in the press that they consume. This is where media relations activity is important. Getting your name mentioned in the right articles, and alongside the right sorts of competitors, can cement your place in the market.

Research people who blog about your area of interest. Comment on and share their material to draw their attention to you.

WORKED EXAMPLE: VA-VOOM!

Because the VA-Voom! team had created a paper that addressed the needs of critical third parties, they already had excellent material to generate some Awareness amongst appropriate third parties. By adapting the content in the paper, they were able to secure guest posts and article slots with various online publications targetting people in human resources and finance.

To generate wider word of mouth they decided to capitalise on a seasonal peak in attention on personal effectiveness and personal goals, in the form of New Year's resolutions in January. They appointed an experienced PR consultant to work with them on this, and together they designed and commissioned some independent research that assessed how much people feel they've reached their potential in the previous year. The data this generates can be cut by region, sector, seniority, etc. This was highly effective because it could be used to create regional and sectoral news releases. To ensure that there was a Funnel in place for this Tap, they made the full research findings available on the website each January. Alongside this they provided a 'next step' of an invitation to enter a competition to win one of ten copies of 'Your Best Year Yet!' by Jenny Ditzler. All competition entrants were asked to opt-in to the VA-Voom! newsletter and received a follow-up email inviting them to the next monthly web seminar, *Making Time to Meet Your Potential*. They re-run this activity each year. Designing this campaign kicked off loads of ideas for running a set of workshops, online and offline, to actually work through Jenny Ditzler's three-day programme with clients and prospects. They decided to monitor performance from the initial Awareness through to sales later in the year, and then add this additional campaign element into their activity if it is successful and as budgets allow.

In your workbook

- Endorsements and testimonials

- Encouraging referrals

- Handling negative feedback

- Complementary companies

- Your media list

- Case study checklist

Facts and figures – where's the evidence?

Sometimes the good opinion of a highly trusted individual can actually shortcut the need to present lots of factual material. Their word is good enough. But usually, and especially in more considered purchases, a buyer will want to tick the logical boxes on their list of buying criteria. This information has to be available. Even if people don't read it in full, they will feel reassured that the information is there should they want it. The five logical bases we looked at in customer service are a great place to start.

> *Even if people don't read it in full, they will feel reassured that the information is there should they want it.*

For every promise you make, you need to provide some proof, for example:

Logical Bases	Likely Question	Possible Proof Points
Cost	Is this value for money?	• ROI calculations • Case studies from similar businesses *Customer feedback shows a 60% increase in productivity*
Speed	Is this a good use of my time? How long will it take?	• Case studies from similar businesses • Average delivery times or payback periods *95% of customers are up and running in just three days*
Quality	Does it meet my standards?	• Industry accreditation, industry standard quality mark • Industry awards *We meet ISO9000 quality standards* *Last year this product won the XYZ Industry Award*
Functionality	Does this solve my problem?	• Case studies from similar businesses • Customer or third party reviews *90% of customers give our product a 5-star rating* *XYZ Body rate our service an 'excellent'*
Dependability	Will it keep working?	• Customer satisfaction scores • Service statistics, e.g. average downtime *Last month our average client satisfaction was rated at 4.5 out of 5* *Last year our service was live for 98% of the time*

Find a proof point to match against each of the logical bases of decision-making and for every promise you make.

Of all these, it's evidence of other happy clients that tops the list. Case studies are a Watertight Marketing must-have. To really stand up to scrutiny the customers featured in the case studies need to be identifiable. Even better, contactable. I'm not saying you need to publish their contact details on your website, but providing the details of customers who are happy to have people ask about their use of your services is enormously persuasive. Buyers may not actually do this, but the fact that you're comfortable for them to do so speaks volumes.

Providing the details of customers who are happy to have people ask about their use of your services is enormously persuasive.

For every product, service or sector, find and publish a case study.

Another way to really prove your mettle is to offer a guarantee. This logical stage in the buying process is about mitigating risk. The buyer wants to know that if they hand over their cash, they will get what they need. Offering a totally genuine money-back guarantee can take most of the risk out of a purchase. It proves your confidence. And, if you're completely confident in what you offer, which of course you should be, then offering a guarantee shouldn't be a scary thing to consider.

WORKED EXAMPLE: VA-VOOM!

Looking back through their records, VA-Voom! found that they were able calculate the number of hours they've saved clients. They decided to make this a cornerstone of their evidence. They added a counter to their website that clocks up the time they've saved people. Because they started to collect data on clients earnings they could assess roughly what their time was worth to output an average hourly value of a typical client. This came in at £100 per hour. By multiplying this by the number of hours worked by assistants, and deducting marketing material. This also enabled them to personalise this financial calculation as part of the *Time Saver Analyser*, and use it in the *Time Saver Audit* so that when a proposal was put to a prospect the cost was always put in context of the hourly value of that individual.

Another key piece of evidence was how satisfied clients were with their service. To demonstrate this they added live feed of the current client satisfaction rating on their website for all new prospects to see as proof of the quality of their service. And, of course, the case studies that they invested in, and budgeted to maintain, was excellent evidence for their prospects to review.

In your workbook

- Your proof audit

- Proof points

- Case study checklist

Having worked up through this process, you have significantly increased the chances of people making it all the way through their buying decision with your company. Keep your core marketing tasks in mind. When it comes to your Funnels, you're looking to **be proven** and **be helpful**. If you have these tasks covered, it's time to tell the world about it.

Your Watertight Funnels Checklist

Step	Leak	Think about
EVALUATION BE PROVEN	**6** NO PROOF	*What do people say about you?* • Endorsements • Affiliates • Referrals *Where's the evidence?* • Facts and figures • Case studies • Guarantee
TRIAL BE HELPFUL	**5** NO CRITICAL APPROVAL	*Who can say no?* • Reaching third parties • Equip for internal selling
	4 NO GATEWAY	*Is there a tiered path to payment?* • Product ladder • No-commitment trial

---

Further reading:

- **Jefferson, S. and Tanton, S. (2013)** *Valuable Content Marketing: How to Make Quality Content the Key to Your Business Success*, **Kogan Page**

- **Scott, D. M. (2011) 3rd ed.** *The New Rules of Marketing & PR*, **John Wiley & Sons**

- **Tovey, D. (2012)** *Principled Selling: How to Win More Business Without Selling Your Soul* **Kogan Page**

- **Townsend, H. (2011)** *FT Guide to Business Networking: How to Use the Power of Online and Offline Networking for Business Success*, **Pearson**

Now, turn your Taps on

When you find a Tap that works it can be tempting to run it at full pelt. A smarter approach is to have a number of Taps generating a steady, and predictable, flow. This means that when one dries up, another can be adjusted. It also means that you have time to tweak your systems downstream to make sure you're ready for what's coming. A deluge of new business can seem like a nice problem to have. But, in an increasingly connected world, there's nowhere to hide if you get a soaking. And, once spilt, water – like a person's good opinion – is tough to channel uphill.

Now we get to what most people think of as marketing. That is generating **Awareness** of, and **Interest** in, what you have on offer. Having ensured that your Bucket holds water, and you have Funnels in place, it's now worth spending money turning the Taps on. But not sooner.

This means that Taps should be no more than third on your list of areas to address as part of a Watertight Marketing operation.

You want to make sure that as much of the outlay you invest turns into profitable sales at the end of the day. This means that Taps should be no more than third on your list of areas to address as part of a Watertight Marketing operation. Have I said this before? Yes, I have. And, I'll say it again before we're done. More than once in fact!

When you do come to tell the world about your business, you'll need to answer the following questions in order to plug the remaining seven profit leaks.

Leak #7 – Information overload – Knowing that you exist is one thing; wanting to find out more is quite another. To draw people into a conversation with you think about:

- Invitation information – *is it worth five minutes?*

Leak #8 – Not representing your business <u>how</u> they're looking – If people can't, or don't want to, engage with your materials you have a surefire way of missing out on their business. Avoid this by considering:

- Multiple formats – *can they digest information as they want to?*

Leak #9 – Not represented <u>where</u> they're looking – Having materials in the right format is great, but only if you show up where they're looking. Think about:

- Showing up – *are you everywhere they turn?*

Leak #10 – Not there <u>when</u> they're looking – There are moments in time when a person is receptive to your message; miss them and you miss the sale. This is about:

- Your moment – *have you got your timing right?*

Leak #11 – Not known by <u>who</u> they ask – In those moments, it's often not you they turn to, but somebody else. For this you need:

- Word of mouth – *are you mentioned by other people?*

Leak #12 – Not known for <u>what</u> you do – If in that moment, what's said about your business isn't quite right, you'll be off the list before they've even started to really think about it. This means addressing:

- Your message – *what are you talking about?*

Leak #13 – No emotional impact – You are competing for a person's attention. Appealing to their innate human responses can be the best way to get noticed. Think about:

- Getting noticed – *does it grab their attention?*

There's a lot to think about here. So to simplify this, maybe even into something you can put on the wall above your desk to keep focussed, you'll be introduced to the concept of The Awareness Equation.

The Awareness Equation

This is a powerful formula that you've understood since you were a small child. Mark Mason, then Managing Director of advertising agency, Mason Zimbler, captured this knowledge in what he calls The Awareness Equation. Applying it to your marketing is extremely effective. Let's remind you how it works.

$$\text{FREQUENCY x IMPACT} = \text{AWARENESS}$$

If I told you something that fundamentally changed your world, something that took the breath from your lungs and made your heart beat out of your chest – I'm willing to bet that I would only need to tell you once. However, when you were learning your times tables at school, repetition was key. This is our equation at work. The first example is low frequency coupled with high impact. The latter is high frequency with low impact.

High impact, in a marketing setting, is about getting an emotional response. This is often achieved with an investment in stunning creative work. An example that comes to mind is the Sony Bravia ad with bouncing coloured balls rolling down a San Francisco street to the haunting sounds of José González. Fear and humour are also examples of this. By triggering an emotional response, lower frequency is sufficient to get noticed.

By triggering an emotional response, lower frequency is sufficient to get noticed.

Low impact with high frequency is often (but not always) used in commodity markets. I can't imagine anyone in the UK not knowing the 'GoCompare' jingle. And, that's not because it's a truly earth-shattering piece of music – it's because it has been played in nearly every commercial break on every TV channel for about the last two years. I like to call this attrition marketing; it wears you down. But, it works.

You need to master this equation if you're going to be remembered. Most businesses don't have the cash for the sort of creative concepts that stop you in your tracks; or the buying power to bag every ad slot going. So, you'll almost certainly need to go for medium frequency and medium impact. The point is that you need both.

Keeping this equation in mind, let's look at the remaining seven profit leaks.

Leak #7 – Information overload

Invitation information – is it worth five minutes?

This is a pretty simple idea in principle. But, often overlooked in practice. Your buyer is busy. You need to make it worth their while to dip into your material. This is the impact part of our equation at work. When someone is busy, the best way to have an impact is to offer something highly relevant to what they're busy doing. You can increase your relevance by being helpful or by being entertaining. Nailing both is really powerful.

> *When someone is busy, the best way to have an impact is to offer something highly relevant to what they're busy doing.*

If you can help someone, with something related to your area expertise, in just five minutes, you're onto a winner. Think about what they'll be asking, or needing to do, in the early stages of their buying decision, and help them with it. The most visited page on the site of my consulting business is the blog post 'How to write a marketing brief'. That's because this is often exactly what someone is doing at this stage in their search for a marketing supplier. You're looking for information that invites people to engage with it. The most powerful materials at this stage in the process are those that take about the same amount of time to read as it does to drink a cup of tea. For example:

- Provide quick answers to questions they may have in their mind.

- Provide tools or checklists to help them draw up their brief or shortlist of potential suppliers.

 Create a set of helpful resources that can be dipped into by a buyer in less than five minutes.

WORKED EXAMPLE: VA-VOOM!

VA-Voom! already had a blog, but only the two founders were posting to it. They were doing this as and when they found time and on subjects that came to mind. The key decision they made to help them generate consistent levels of Awareness was to be more structured in their approach to blogging. The first action was to include the assistants as authors on the blog. This added variety and personality, but it also shared the workload making it possible to commit to posting something new every week. With more people on the blogging team, they became able to bounce ideas around. They decided to put aside a two-hour slot once per quarter to brainstorm and create a blog calendar. Then, they introduced a 10-minute session each week to review what was on-plan to see if it was still relevant and add in anything responsive if they needed to. At the first session, they came up with this first month of blog titles:

- Is it cost-effective to use a virtual assistant?

- How to get the most from working with a virtual assistant

- 10 ways to save 10 minutes every day

- How do I get more stuff done?

- Counting the cost of doing your own admin.

The other reason people may give you some of their valuable time, is because you arouse their curiosity, or make your materials entertaining. You can do this with humour, controversy or simply presenting information in an interesting way. You can often take people's common objections as the starting point for this kind of material, and then present compelling arguments to win people around.

Used well, cartoons and jokes can also get people interested in your ideas. The great thing about pulling this off in your marketing materials, is that it's the sort of thing that travels well in social media.

WORKED EXAMPLE: VA-VOOM!

Having come up with the really straightforward ideas, they then worked on some more thought-provoking ones. They came up with these ideas:

- 10 ways to waste time and achieve nothing

- Being busy means you're important, right?

- What would you do with another you?

- Is being good at admin something you'll be proud of on your death bed?

- Delegation is for wimps.

To add to the range for formats, and to show a little more personality, VA-Voom! decided to get a cartoon drawn each month poking gentle fun at being overworked, stressed or typical procrastination techniques.

In your workbook

- Great questions

- Tea time challenge

- Is it relevant?

Leak #8 – Not representing your business for <u>how</u> they're looking

Multiple formats – can they digest information as they want to?

Different people like to consume information in different ways. My father-in-law buys a slew of broadsheet newspapers everyday. I catch up with the headlines on the radio in the morning and get updates via Twitter throughout the day. It's likely that we'll find some of the same information, but the way we consume it is different. The same is true in a corporate setting. Some people will read their monthly trade magazines, others might hop onto a website to watch a video briefing. You need to make sure that your information is presented in the format, or most likely formats, that your buyers tend to use.

> *You don't need to worry too much about presenting the same information in multiple formats.*

You don't need to worry too much about presenting the same information in multiple formats. Some people may encounter the material a number of times. This just increases the frequency, and thereby your chances of being noticed. However, if amongst your chosen formats there isn't at least one that you know your buyer uses, you'll miss the frequency part of the equation altogether as your message doesn't stand a chance of being received.

 Run a study that tracks how your buyers engage with different information sources whilst choosing what you sell.

In practice, this means that you shouldn't dismiss the more traditional formats, like print. Even with the Internet nearing universal access in most developed countries, and tablet devices making onscreen reading more pleasurable, many people will choose to print the information they want. This is especially true if it needs their careful attention. Whether in a consumer or business context, they may want to sit in a quiet corner, take it with them on a train, or make some notes on it. For some markets ignoring printed materials is ignoring the needs of some really important people. In business, for example, the more senior the decision maker, the more likely they are to digest printed material. Many PAs will still prepare a pack of reading material each morning for a Chief Executive to read whilst travelling, for example. Whilst ignoring traditional formats is a common error, the converse is also true. With more and more people accessing materials on smartphone or tablet devices, you need to be equally mindful of how your content appears on these. If your audience includes heavy users of these technologies, you will need to look at investing in responsive web design.

 Always test how your web pages look when viewed on the types of devices your audience commonly uses and when someone presses 'print'.

CASE STUDY: Connect Assist

Connect Assist, providers of online and telephone support services for the third sector, has Chief Executives firmly in mind. Over a 12-month period the company focused on key themes, for which they produced a quarterly discussion paper and round-table events. Patrick Nash, Chief Executive, comments, "I've been a charity Chief Executive, and I know that I just would not have sat in front of my screen reading supplier information. The best time I get for reflection, or reading around my subject, is on the train. And, the same is true for our potential buyers." With this in mind, careful attention gets paid to produce materials that looked good when printed off at their end. Blog posts, social media, direct mail, and email were used to drive people to the content, but they knew that it would be consumed offline. Patrick continues, "I know it's worked, not only because of click rates, but because of the quality of the conversations I've had. They haven't just downloaded it; they've read it." The company exceeded its growth targets by 14% in the period of this activity. What's more, this growth was achieved in the toughest economic circumstances this industry has seen in decades.

So, you need to make sure the obvious ways people interact with your material are catered for. But, don't shy away from being a little more daring. There seem to be more formats to consider by the day. Digital formats are increasingly important. Video, for example, is growing in popularity. YouTube is now the starting point for as many web journeys as almost any search engine. Alternative formats give you fantastic opportunities to inform and inspire people. Whether it's a video tutorial, a podcast, a smartphone app, a beautiful infographic, or a live web seminar – there's no excuse for presenting

Alternative formats give you fantastic opportunities to inform and inspire people.

your information in dull or soulless ways. Indeed, thinking creatively can make your message stand out. When I was at University in the late 1990s, the National Union of Students in the UK ran a highly effective sexual health awareness campaign by stickering 10p pieces and distributing them around union clubs and bars. The fact that I can still recall the campaign shows how well this worked. Interesting formats can contribute to the Impact part of the equation.

 Consider how your buyers engage with their leisure activities, like music, books, games, etc. This will give you format ideas to show some personality.

CASE STUDY: ShipServ

ShipServ, an online marketplace for the maritime industry, tripled its revenue in three years in part by matching their marketing to their buyers' thinking. Unlike media companies or youth brands, using video and social media was really breaking the mould for this market. John Watton, former Marketing Director, comments, "We knew that getting a sense of personality across was essential to getting people to trust our business. So many companies in our industry seemed faceless and distant, and with rapid growth and a global market, it would have been easy to go the same way." One of the company's most successful activities was a simple video interview with the company founder about how and why he set up the business. Using a Vimeo channel, they used this as part of a range of video that employed humour and personality to show what ShipServ was all about. In the first quarter of introducing video content they achieved over 600 views. Making information available in these sorts of formats, within the context of an integrated marketing operation that supported every step of the buying decision, contributed to an increase of sales-ready leads of 400%.

When considering the range of formats you use, the following breakdown is really useful. From a practical perspective, this gives you six different types of format. To ensure you have a range that appeals to different users you may wish to issue a new piece in each format each week over a rolling six-week programme.

	Physical	Digital
Written	Papers, Brochures, Books, etc.	Blog, Presentation slides, etc.
Visual	3-dimensional direct mail (Ie.g. a pop-up), Posters, Murals, etc.	Infographic, Cartoons, Imagery, Interactive online animations, etc.
Aural	In-person presentation, Events, etc.	Video, Podcast, etc.

CASE STUDY: Fable Trading

Trollbeads, the collectible jewellery brand, is a highly visual product. As such, Fable Trading, the UK & Ireland distributor, invests in stunning original photography to use on their website, in-store promotions and advertising. To make additional use of this investment, and to engage their buyers in another way, they use their photography to make a digital desktop calendar available to download each month. This puts their product in sight of their buyers every time they log in to their computers, and encourages them to look at a new selection from the range each month.

WORKED EXAMPLE: VA-VOOM!

Across the new activities that VA-Voom! decided to put in place, they covered a number of bases in terms of format variety. Their new mix of activity included:

- Blog articles that they post online

- Video tips that they upload to YouTube and embed on their website

- Their core paper, *The Real the Cost of Self-Administration,* can be downloaded and printed

- This paper is also available as audio recording to allow people to digest it when travelling

- A cartoon that they post on their blog, which they then share as a Twitpic and pin on Pinterest

- A simple direct mail letter that incorporates the cartoon and directs people online

- Their monthly live web seminar

- Regular attendance at relevant networking events

- An actual 3-dimensional book that they use as direct mail for high value prospects.

Their web pages also look great when people press print. Longer term, they're going to consider getting a smartphone app created, and when they refresh their website in a few years time, they'll make sure it is built with responsive design for various devices.

In your workbook

- Format ideas

Leak #9 – Not represented <u>where</u> they're looking

Showing up – are you everywhere they turn?

The effect you're aiming for is for a buyer to think "Wow, I keep seeing XYZ Ltd everywhere, I must check them out". This is particularly important if your market requires some education to see the need for what you have to offer. For this, you'll really need to up the Frequency of your marketing.

The ideal scenario goes something like this:

1. They see an article about you in a trade magazine.

2. They're chatting to a trusted contact about something related to your area of expertise, and that person says they should check you out.

3. A Tweet of yours shows up in their timeline because it's been shared by someone they follow, which they now notice and click because of the two earlier instances... you're now on their radar and it's your job to keep them interested.

In this example there were three touches before they took any action. It's said that most people need at least three exposures to a message to receive it. In market and scientific research, seeing the same result from three different sources is often used to determine that it is truly relevant. It's called 'triangulation'. To put this to effect in marketing your business, you need to select at least three ways of getting your message out. And, you need to commit to continuing with them even if you can't directly correlate enquiries to all three. Because, as shown in the example above, only the last click would have shown up in your statistics. But, without the other exposures to your company, the click wouldn't have happened at all.

> *To put this to effect in marketing your business, you need to select at least three ways of getting your message out.*

CASE STUDY: Mubaloo

Mobile phone app developers, Mubaloo, where Mark Mason is now Chief Executive, work hard to maintain their market presence. They use multiple channels, from traditional business awards, direct mail postcards, to the latest social media. And, they're committed to a consistent level of marketing activity alongside natural peaks in their industry. He comments, "People often say that 'we're everywhere they look', which means we're always on a buyer's radar. We're yet to hear of a big app being developed in our space for which we weren't considered."

Where above we looked at providing a range of formats to allow people to engage with your materials in a way that suits each buyer, here we're talking about how they access that material. It's about finding ways, or channels, for putting the material in front of them.

 Choose at least three different channels for each audience to maximise the power of triangulation.

WORKED EXAMPLE: VA-VOOM!

The range of regular activities, detailed above, that VA-Voom! put into place ensured that triangulation was possible across online and offline channels, where they now frequently show-up with similar messages. The three channels that they prioritised for consistent use were LinkedIn, Twitter and third party websites.

 In your workbook

- Can you triangulate?

Leak #10 – Not represented <u>when</u> they're looking

Your moment – have you got your timing right?

We saw in chapter four how developing a range of time-chunked materials will help you to earn the right to increasing durations of a person's time. Once you have these materials in place, you need to master what I've taken to calling Three S Timing:

- Selectivity

- Scheduling

- Seasonality.

 You'll often find that a customer reports that winning their business was a result of 'lucky timing'. That is, you happened to show up when they were looking for what you sell. Luck has very little to do with this. What's actually going on here is *selectivity*. And, it's where marketing frequency is absolutely essential.

Have you ever noticed how when you learn a new word, it seems to crop up on the news, in the book you're reading, or in conversation with a friend? It was always there, you just didn't notice it. The same is true when you're on the look out for a new car, you'll suddenly see the model you have in mind passing you at every turn or parked next to you at the supermarket. This is a trick of the mind. To enjoy the fruits of 'lucky timing', your company needs to crop up when a person happens to be thinking about what you're selling. Which, effectively, means being there all the time. To do this, you need to commit to a number of regular marketing activities rather than one-offs, or big bang campaigns. The frequency of these will depend on buying cycles in your industry. What you're aiming for is to act a little like a lighthouse, with a beacon flashing regularly enough to be seen at the right moment.

> *To enjoy the fruits of 'lucky timing', your company needs to crop up when a person happens to be thinking about what you're selling.*

Commit to a small number of regular marketing activities. For example, a weekly blog, a monthly newsletter and quarterly direct mail.

CASE STUDY: Comet Global Consulting

When Comet Global Consulting, customer technology specialists, were looking for some strategic marketing support, one of their directors recommended my consulting business. I had worked with him for about six months when I was in corporate marketing some three years earlier, and we had connected on LinkedIn. He had never signed up for a newsletter, or clicked on a blog. There was nothing to say he knew anything about my new business. Every week (without fail) I update my LinkedIn status with my latest blog post. This had the effect of just popping up in this buyer's newsfeed regularly enough to express what I do. When it came to needing what I offer, he finally clicked on a link. But, without the previous 150-odd updates, he may not have noticed this one.

With a commitment to a steady stream of ongoing activities, you can further increase your chances of showing up at the right time by understanding and matching your buyers' work patterns and *scheduling* your communications to match. Mapping a typical day, week and year for your buyers will help you to work out when to get in touch. For example, Mondays and Fridays probably aren't best for your direct mail to arrive with a business person. And, calling a consumer at home during working hours is pretty futile.

 Use scheduling tools to maintain a presence outside normal office hours. If you need to respond in these times, think about using a call-handling service.

There's also *seasonality* to consider. Even if you're not an ice-cream vendor, there will be seasonality in your market. Financial year-ends, school holidays, industry events, funding cycles and the like, can all lead to seasonal changes in demand. Map things that happen over the course of a year that you could talk about or help with. There will be events that happen every year, like getting your tax return in on time, and there will be one-offs in that year specifically, like a big sporting event. The former should be worked into your ongoing marketing plan, the latter should form part of your specific 12-month plan. There may also be dated triggers that relate to an individual or specific company, like renewal dates, that would allow you to time your communications perfectly.

 If you collect key data, like year-end or birthdays, when people sign up for your email newsletter, you can set up automated emails to go them at these times. MailChimp includes this feature in its 'forever free' account.

WORKED EXAMPLE: VA-VOOM!

As well as covering office hours on a daily basis, VA-Voom! decided to ensure that a certain number of social media updates were scheduled for early mornings, evenings and weekends to catch busy people working at these time.

They reviewed their blog calendar to include a post about dealing with the extra workload either side of a holiday scheduled around public holidays, and they added a note to their 12-month plan to highlight this in their social media and email marketing in the run-up to national holidays each year. They also scheduled to write a post with ideas for keeping children entertained in holidays, and one about freeing up precious time to spend with children.

To really hook into seasonality right through to actual sales these they added a signpost to pieces of content with next steps through to services that support typical administrative hotspots in a person's working year, for example:

- Getting the Christmas card list updated and cards sent

- Organising the office Chistmas party

- Setting their annual budgets.

In your workbook

- Frequency checklist

- A Day in the Life

- A Week in the Life

- A Year in the Life

Leak #11 – Not known by <u>who</u> they ask

Word of mouth – are you mentioned by other people?

When people are thinking of buying something, they will often ask around to see if someone they know can recommend a supplier. If you've empowered your customers as referrers, enquiries should be coming your way. And, at Leak #5, there are people that your buyer will want, or need, to consult before they make the final purchasing decision. However, here at the Awareness stage, you're looking for more than customers and people directly influencing the purchase to know who you are. This is word of mouth.

Word of mouth is a broader concept than a referral, which is a person directed into your Funnels by a third party a little way down their decision. And, it's wider than influencing influencers. An influencer is consciously consulted by the buyer. Word of mouth is more about creating a background hum. It has an almost subconscious effect. The information comes *to* them, rather than being sought out *by* them. From a casual comment in which your company is mentioned over lunch with a trusted contact, to seeing an interesting question of yours shared in social media. It's the Frequency side of our equation at work again. To create word of mouth, you need to get people talking about your company.

> *Word of mouth is more about creating a background hum. It has an almost subconscious effect.*

You can do this by hooking into conversations that are already happening, or being the initiator. Pertinent ways to do this are:

- **Ask thought-provoking questions:** asking good questions shows intelligence and invites people to respond. You can post these in social media, or have them in the back of your mind for appropriate moments at a networking event.

- **Start a debate:** come at a topic from the reverse perspective, can you argue both sides of a debate. Putting out a discussion paper that looks at both sides of a tricky subject can be really compelling.

- **Say something controversial:** you shouldn't do this simply for the sake of it, but if your company has some strong core beliefs or values, you can afford to be forthright about it.

- **Ride a common theme:** find perennial topics that come up in your industry about which you can have an opinion or provide useful insights.

 Research any #subject on Twitter that relate to your area of expertise to see and join in on what's being discussed on a particular topic.

 In your workbook

- Conversation starters

WORKED EXAMPLE: VA-VOOM!

As soon as the VA-Voom! blog started using headlines, and posed questions, designed to get people thinking the click throughs and social sharing improved. The team was also encouraged and trained in using these to spark conversation in LinkedIn groups and at networking events. Their annual survey and PR activity on meeting your true potential hooks into existing conversations had in January about New Year's Resolutions and planning the year ahead. The poll seeks to prove the hypothesis that a large percentage of people do not feel they are meeting their true potential which provides stand-out headlines, like '9 out of 10 business leaders were disappointed with what they managed to achieve in the last twelve months'.

Leak #12 – Not known for <u>what</u> you do

Your message – what are you talking about?

Messaging is about Impact. But, more specifically relevance. The more relevant something is, the more impact it has. However stunning, or thought-provoking, a piece is on the subject of fly-fishing locations in the USA, for example, I will just never take a second look. If there was a truly stunning visual that my emotional brain couldn't ignore, I might take a first glance. But, in my busy life, I would simply flick passed the article itself, because I don't enjoy fishing or live in the USA. You need to make your message, particularly at the Awareness and Interest stages, highly relevant to the people you're talking to. Having impact is one thing, having the right kind of impact is another. You don't want to generate the wrong sort of work.

> *Having impact is one thing, having the right kind of impact is another.*

There is a right kind and a wrong kind of work for any business. If your marketing isn't up to scratch you can find yourself in a bit of a vicious cycle of doing the wrong kind, which in turn leads to more of it. To determine which is which, ask yourself what of the work you do takes you forward, and what holds you back?

Work that holds you back will look something like this:

- It's not the most profitable use of the resources used in delivering it.

- You wouldn't shout about it.

- It's not helping you to learn, or hone, valuable skills.

- Your team don't actually want to do it.

Conversely, the right kind of work is:

- The most profitable use of the resources you have.

- You'd enter it for awards, case study it and talk about it in sales meetings.

- It's using skills that you know are in high demand.

- Your team actively enjoy doing it – it's the kind of stuff they'd tell their friends about or put on their CV.

- Shouting about this sort of work would help you attract great employees.

It's not unusual, especially in the early stages of your business, to find that at least a proportion of your work is not quite ticking all of these boxes. In fact, you probably need to go through a bit of this whilst you work out what your real strengths are. But, there comes a point where you need to be more discerning about what your business does, and does not, offer.

Doing the wrong sort of work is damaging. In terms of Awareness, this is often compounded because you're talking about the stuff that you're doing – but don't want to do – and more people keep coming to you for that. If you're not crystal clear about what you do, you'll generate random enquiries. These eat time, and can lead you down various blind alleys, cluttering your message and making it difficult for people to really understand what it is you offer. The more cluttered your message, the less impact you have.

> *If you're not crystal clear about what you do, you'll generate random enquiries.*

WORKED EXAMPLE: VA-VOOM!

The VA-Voom! management team ran an internal workshop to assess the tasks that their people enjoy and don't enjoy doing to help them work out what to talk loudly about. They found:

- A task that clients often ask VA-Voom! to undertake is credit control and bookkeeping. They can and will do this with a smile. But most of their assistants fed back that they don't actively enjoy it. So, it's not something they specifically highlight.

- Conversely, inbox management and social media scheduling is something that a number of assistants said they'd become highly adept at and really enjoy doing, so this now features large in their marketing.

You need to make sure that people don't just know you, but that they know you for the right thing. Sticking to a tight set of messages at the Awareness stage helps you with this. You don't want to generate loads of enquiries, simply to spend time and energy turning people away or taking on work that holds you back.

 If you're using Google AdWords, make sure the broad-match settings aren't displaying your ads for things you don't do, and use negative keywords to be even more targetted.

CASE STUDY: Halo Media

Halo Media is a design company in Bristol. They undertake brand, advertising and digital media projects for consumer- and business-facing companies. They work in a crowded and highly competitive market. When they refreshed their own website, they deliberately went for arresting visuals. Their site uses Graffiti-style illustration, iconography and bold clashing colours.

It's the kind of design that you either love or hate. Their rationale is that you can't appeal to everyone and you shouldn't try. Managing Director, Nick Ellis, comments, "If you are so concerned with 'fitting in' to the industry you're not concentrating on what makes you special and most importantly what excites and interests you. We wanted to attract clients who share our love of aesthetics and want to do stimulating work. Our website sets out our stall clearly, without the need to explain why we're different or what drives our agency. It's right in front of you on the home page. As a result our website captures the essence of Halo and we look like no one else." As a direct result of this bold visual approach, they started to win more, and more profitable, work from the kind of clients they love working with. One such client was Unilever. The site has the effect of filtering out anyone who isn't likely to enjoy working with them, meaning that the enquiries they receive are from the right kind of client. The agency credits their new website, and the follow-up thereafter, with tripling their turnover. This is an achievement all the more impressive given that it was undertaken in an economic downturn.

What often happens, particularly as businesses start to engage in social media, is that they lose focus on what they're talking about. Once you know what you offer, and to whom, stick to it.

We're all interested in lots of things, and have opinions on them. But, when it comes to getting your message across, saying less (more often) means it is more likely to stick. We saw the power of triangulation earlier. This only works if it is, broadly, the same message each time. So, if you offer marketing services, don't keep sharing articles about human resources or accountancy. However interesting or well-written they might be, it just won't help people to understand what *you* do. That's not to say that your business should sound like a stuck record. You can vary the angle from which you come at a subject and talk around the edges, but you do need to stay broadly on topic. And, of course you should be coming at the topic from an empathetic perspective in the first place. The most effective way of keeping on track with your messaging is to limit yourself to a maximum of three core themes, within a broad area of expertise.

CASE STUDY: Ascentor

Information risk consultants, Ascentor, targets medium-sized businesses for whom information security is likely to start becoming more important. Their broad area of expertise is Information Security. Their three themes are:

- Securing your information strengthens your business

- Information risk is not an IT issue

- Information risk is a matter of context.

Dave James, Managing Director, comments, "Having our themes in place makes it much easier to plan things like our blog content. If what's been suggested underpins one of these themes we use it, if not, we don't."

However, you also need to be mindful of not coming across as a bore. It's absolutely fine for you and your team to show your personalities and share some of the lighter things in life. In fact it's more than fine, as we saw in Leak #3, making a human connection is really important. Just don't make other areas of interest the basis for the majority of your conversations.

 Set up Google Reader, or other RSS feed tool, to pull all the relevant third content into one place for you to review, share and comment on.

To illustrate this, let's imagine the Twitter timelines of two small business marketing consultants. One where followers would be forgiven for being unsure what you do, and one where it's crystal clear.

Confused timeline...	Clear timeline...
Just finishing off my bookkeeping. I'll be glad when it's done.	Just off to conduct a #marketing audit for a great little IT company. Looking forward to this one.
RT @somebody: Three tips for a smooth office relocation - url.com	*NEW POST* '10 ways in which #marketing is like exercise' - url.com
NEW POST '10 ways in which marketing is like exercise' - url.com	RT @somebody: How to get the best from a #marketing consultant - url.com <~ good tips here
RT @someoneelse: How to calculate the size of the universe <~ wow, fascinating	It's @somebody's birthday today, look what we got her - url.com
Press archive: Making marketing work harder in small businesses - url.com via @publicationx	Press archive: Making #marketing work harder in small businesses - url.com via @publicationx
We're enjoying some sunshine here today. Is the sun shining on you too?	RT @someoneelse: Tips for your small business newsletter <~ really useful advice #marketing #email
Phew, glad it's Friday. Looking forward to a bit of hill climbing this weekend.	Happy Friday everybody. Hope you have fabulous weekends planned.
Happy Monday people. What's on your list for the week?	Hello Monday. Is it a #marketing Monday for any of you?

About 80% of what you chat about in online and traditional networking should be broadly connected to what your business actually does.

WORKED EXAMPLE: VA-VOOM!

The VA-Voom! broad area of expertise was Personal Effectiveness. Within this they brainstormed and agreed on the following three themes:

- Make time to meet your potential

- Success means focussing on what you're good at

- You should manage your to-do list, it shouldn't manage you.

To keep the whole team in touch with great third party material in the right subject area, they set up a Google Reader that everyone uses into which they've run the feeds of various websites and bloggers in their area of expertise.

For some businesses, the company name itself can contribute to misunderstanding of what they actually do. As you're already in business, I'm guessing you have a company name in place. It can be worth taking a moment to consider whether that name is helpful in terms of getting people to understand what you do. There are broadly three approaches, each with their own pros and cons:

- **Descriptive company names:** this is something that firmly anchors your company in a discipline and often a geography too. Something like 'Bristol Sports Trophies' – it tells people what you do and where you do it. This is crystal clear for its primary purpose, but might cause a problem if this business wanted to expand beyond Bristol and sell anything other than sports trophies.

- **Conceptual company names:** this is something a bit more creative and can give you a chance to express a little more personality. My consulting business is called 'Clear Thought'. This gives a sense of what it might be like to work with me, but it doesn't tell you that it's marketing I think clearly about. It would allow me to expand my services if I wanted to, perhaps into Clear Thought HR, IT, Finance, etc. Many big brands have highly conceptual names, like Orange, Apple, Google. There's no clue to what they do in the name. This is helpful to business expansion, but harder to get people to immediately understand what you do. It's also worth noting that if your brand name is an actual word in the dictionary, rather than one exclusive to you, it can be difficult to track what's being said about you in social platforms. Apple and Orange must see lots of discussions about fruit!

Apple and Orange must see lots of discussions about fruit!

- **Founder names or initials:** the name of the person who founded a business doesn't give a sense of the business, neither does it describe what you do. That's not to say that you can't be successful taking this approach, Marks & Spencer and many more prove this. It can, however, take a long time and a lot of money, to get any significance associated with otherwise meaningless words. It can also make it harder for that founder to exit the business down the line if some of the brand walks out of the door with them.

The best way to bridge the gap between something conceptual and something descriptive is to have an interplay between the company name and a strap line. Where possible I'd go for a name that is catchy and expresses some of your personality, and a strap line that tells people what you do. This can also apply to product naming.

CASE STUDY: VPW Systems

Like a lot of small businesses, VPW Systems was named after its founder, Vince Wilton. He named the company when he was working by himself, but the company has now grown and potential customers struggle to know what they do from the business name. To overcome this, but without the difficulty and expense of renaming the company, they added a more descriptive strap line to their logo and materials. They worked with a branding specialist to come up with 'Making IT Easier'. This not only tells people what they do, but also gives an idea of the problem they solve.

> *People will often associate your business with the first thing they hear about you.*

People will often associate your business with the first thing they hear about you, so it's important to find ways of reminding them of other things you might offer. You can really help people understand your full offering with visual devices. This will, of course, depend on what you're selling. You can use this against blog posts, service pages and any other key content to highlight where on your full offer what they're reading sits. It's also important to keep existing customers clued-up. For example, if your customers log in to some sort of control panel to manage their services then the full range needs to be visible, not just what they have bought. The services they don't currently use could be greyed out, with access to compelling sales materials in place of service information. In a knowledge-based business, developing some sort of model can help you to show people the full extent of your services. For my marketing consultancy, I always highlight where on a six-step sales funnel image what I'm talking about pertains to, which shows that my advice covers the whole process.

 Find a visual way of depicting your complete offering and always put what people are reading, buying or using in context of the wider offer.

> ### WORKED EXAMPLE: VA-VOOM!
>
> The VA-Voom! founders were pretty attached to their company name, but took a moment to think about whether it was helpful to clarity of understanding. It had a play on words with the use of VA in the name, and gave a sense of speed, like someone getting something done quickly. The rhythm was almost like someone waving a magic wand. All of this was great and gave no reason to change their company name. But, on reflection, they conceded that you'd only understand the name if you knew that the initials VA stood for Virtual Assistant, and you understood what a virtual assistant does. Working with a branding team, they came up with the strap line *Virtual Assistants. Real Potential.*

In your workbook

- What's right and what's wrong?

- What are you talking about?

- What's in a name?

- Visualise it

Leak #13 – No emotional impact

Getting noticed – does it grab their attention?

You can have tightly welded every one of the last twelve leaks, but if people don't notice you, you're just not even in the running. Remember that for every order that comes your way there is a human being somewhere who made a decision.

We saw in Leak #3 that having an emotional connection is essential for getting a person over the final hurdle to becoming a customer. It's also important at the start of the process. As previously mentioned, a person living in a modern capitalist economy is exposed to as many as 3000 marketing messages every day. That's on top of getting on with their lives. To even know that your company exists a person needs to make space in their brain. To cut through the clutter of thoughts and information that are bombarding people, you need to grab their attention. This is the Impact part of our equation at work. As we saw in chapter three, grabbing a person's attention is most effectively achieved by hooking into their emotions. An emotional response happens to you, rather than being something consciously controlled. If you can trigger an emotional response in your buyer, they can't help but notice you.

> *If you can trigger an emotional response in your buyer, they can't help but notice you.*

In a considered buying decision, it's often an issue or irritation they're looking to resolve. This is about accessing those negative emotions that people want to move away from. Marketers will often ask you to think of the 'point of pain' that your product or service solves. If you went through the thought processes of looking at the problem, and the problem behind the problem in Leak #3, then you should have an idea what this is. In that leak, at the bottom end of the process, you need to evoke positive emotions that enable people to connect with your organisation on a human level. Here, in the top half of the process, you're trying to get people to want to change their current situation by choosing to find out more about your business. You need them to *do* something rather than simply *feel* something. This tends to mean hooking into a negative emotion. You need to create enough discomfort that people want to change something, but not so much as they feel deflated or violated by your message. Once you've found the right hooks, use them for your headlines, Tweets, blog titles, etc.

> *You need them to do something rather than simply feel something.*

 Brainstorm the day-to-day irritations that manifest in your buyers' lives that your product or service would resolve.

WORKED EXAMPLE: VA-VOOM!

The VA-Voom! team decided that appropriate negative emotions to use when thinking of headlines, blog titles and social media activity designed to generate Awareness were:

- Feeling stressed and overworked

- Feeling frustrated at not doing the stuff you want to be doing.

They felt that inappropriate negative emotions would start to veer into therapeutic or counselling territory, for example:

- Signs of depression or anxiety caused by stress

- Relationship problems caused by excessive workloads.

In your workbook

- What's the problem?

When all these suggestions come together for your business, you'll have a steady flow of interested people to talk to. These are the Taps for your business. When putting this guidance into practice keep reminding yourself of what you're trying to achieve. Here, you need to **be there** and **be relevant.**

Your Flowing Taps Checklist

Step	Leak	Think about
AWARENESS BE THERE	**13** NO EMOTIONAL IMPACT	*Why does it matter?* • Emotional hook (problem)
	12 WHAT	*What are you talking about?* • The right kind of work • One theme, three messages • Name and strap line
	11 WHO	*Are you mentioned by other people?* • Word of mouth • Conversation starters
	10 WHEN	*Have you got your timing right?* • Selectivity • Seasonality • Scheduling
	9 WHERE	*Are you everywhere they turn?* • Triangulation
	8 HOW	*Can they digest as they want to?* • Format selection
INTEREST BE RELEVANT	**7** INFORMATION OVERLOAD	*Is it worth five minutes?* • Invitation information

Further reading:

- **For more on the Sony Bravia ad mentioned, please visit:**
  http://theinspirationroom.com/daily/2005/sony-bravia-lcd-screen/

- **Hall, R. (2009)** *Brilliant Marketing: What the Best Marketers Know,*
  Do and Say, **Pearson Education**

- **Jefferson, S. and Tanton, S. (2013)** *Valuable Content Marketing: How*
  to Make Quality Content the Key to Your Business Success,
  Kogan Page

- **Levinson, J. C. (2007)** *Guerilla Marketing: Easy and Inexpensive*
  Strategies for Making Big Profits From Your Small Business,
  Piatkus Books

- **McCandless, D. (2010)** *Information is Beautiful,* **HarperCollins**

- **McFarlan, B. (2003)** *Drop the Pink Elephant: 21 Steps to Personal*
  Communication Heaven, **Capstone Press**

- **Scott, D. M., Halligan, B. and Shah, D. (2009)** *Inbound Marketing:*
  Get Found using Google, Social Media and Blogs, **John Wiley & Sons**

SUMMARY OF PART THREE

The starting point for any business that wants to make a profit is to secure its Bucket. If you can reduce the effort that goes into keeping your coffers topped up it's much easier to move your business forward. The marketing tasks here are to **be consistent** and **be friendly.**

Your three areas of focus are:

- **Leak #1 – Forgotten customers –** Consistent customer communications that proactively address any service needs and keep your business in their minds.

- **Leak #2 – Poor on-boarding –** A structured approach to communication with new customers as they settle into their relationship with you which demonstrate that your service is consistent with the expectations they had.

- **Leak #3 – No emotional connection –** A visual and written style with a personal touch that's friendly and allows people to make an emotional connection with your business.

Once you have a Bucket that holds water, you need to ensure that you have Funnels in place to direct people to it. The marketing tasks here are to **be helpful** and **be proven.**

Again, there are three areas of focus:

- **Leak #4 – No gateway –** A coherent set of products that lead helpfully from one to the next with the inclusion of a stepping stone that allows people to understand what it's like to be a customer before they are one.

- **Leak #5 – No critical approval –** A clear way of educating, or helping your buyer educate, anyone who could veto the purchase decision.

- **Leak #6 – No proof –** A systematic approach to signposting some sort of proof against every promise or claim that you make.

With a Bucket in place and your Funnels at the ready, it's time to turn the Taps on. The marketing tasks you need to keep in mind are to **be relevant** and **be there**.

This is a big subject, in which seven key areas need to be carefully considered:

- **Leak #7 – Information overload –** A steady stream of relevant information that invites people into finding out more.

- **Leak #8 – How –** A range of familiar and novel formats so that people can engage with ease and enjoyment.

- **Leak #9 – Where –** A selection of at least three places to put your materials that you know your potential buyers already access.

- **Leak #10 – When –** A commitment to timing the release of your material so that people are most likely to notice it.

- **Leak #11 – Who –** A way of getting people talking about your business so that buyers hear something good about you regardless of who they turn to.

- **Leak #12 – What –** An absolute clarity of purpose in telling people what your business does.

- **Leak #13 – No emotional impact –** The ability to strike an emotional chord with your potential buyer that means they can't help but notice you and they feel compelled to take action.

With your overall Watertight Marketing framework mapped out from Part Three, this will now act as your checklist for marketing improvements.

PART FOUR

Small businesses are the backbone of our economy. And, small business owners are probably amongst the hardest working people around. As you're reading this, I want you to have your thinking cap on, coming up with ideas for putting this all into action. And, then I want you to make it happen. I want to hear that it's working, delivering long-term sales results for your business. So, let's make that marketing plan one that you can afford!

MAKING IT HAPPEN

Armed with the ideas you've come up with at each step in the process to stem every leak you spotted, you'll now be wanting to put them into action. I'm guessing you don't have limitless funds at your disposal, so you'll need to be smart about where you put your cash. Here, you'll be guided through developing a plan that covers every step in a person's buying decision whilst leaving enough in the pot to respond to changes as they happen.

You'll want to know that your ideas are bearing fruit. To do this, you'll need to pick a set of sensible marketing metrics that build towards your financial targets. Getting this right means also being alert to becoming overly reliant on analysis at the expense of maintaining your company's stand-out qualities.

And, then there's sticking at it. Marketing is like exercise. You'll be challenged to commit to a lifestyle change rather than be tempted by the allure of quick fixes.

Your affordable marketing plan

It's so easy to blow the budget before you've completed the job. Most often, and because most people see marketing as those Taps, the activity plan and budget is loaded onto driving Awareness, leaving nothing in the pot to support a person's decision making all the way through to a sale and beyond. To make sure you have everything covered, you need to map your marketing activity, and spend, against the six tasks of marketing making sure there's a tick in every box.

You need a marketing budget

Whether you're spending a modest or a massive amount on your marketing, taking time to structure your activity plan and marketing budget will help you in a number of important ways:

- You will be able to make sensible decisions about where to spend your money.

- You will be able to track whether your spend is worth it in the long term.

- You will avoid nasty surprises in the form of unexpected costs.

- You'll ensure that you don't run out of cash part way through the year.

- You'll be able to flex your spend strategically and in response to your market.

Many of the businesses I've encountered, particularly at the smaller end of the scale, have an ad hoc approach to marketing expenditure. They simply respond to marketing opportunities as they come along, deciding in that moment whether they have the funds available. At the larger end of the scale the other extreme is often true, with an activity-based budget set at the beginning of the year, with limited scope for flexibility and responsiveness. Both approaches have their pros and cons, but there is a middle ground.

The Watertight Marketing approach to planning and budgeting is split into three fundamental principles:

1. Select an integrated mix of marketing tools and techniques to ensure that every marketing task is fulfilled.

2. Establish an ABC Budget from which you commit to baseline level of spending.

3. Set a sensible contingency from which you can pre-plan how you would flex your marketing spend up or down if you need to.

Joined-up marketing

Your first step in setting your Watertight Marketing plan is to work out what shape it should be. You do this by looking at the mix of marketing activities you're using and working out roughly what level of influence they have against each of the six marketing tasks that support the buying decision.

1. Create a spreadsheet with the six steps in the buying decision down the left hand column.

Step				
AWARENESS				
INTEREST				
EVALUATION				
TRIAL				
ADOPTION				
LOYALTY				

2. Across the top of the columns, list the key areas of marketing spend in your budget. For example:

   - **Public Relations (PR):** to include all your spending on media relations, press releases, etc.

   - **Advertising (AD):** to include all paid-for on and offline advertising.

   - **Social media (SM):** to include social media support, blog writing, etc.

   - **Etc.**

Step	PR	AD	SM	Etc.	Etc.	Etc.
AWARENESS						
INTEREST						
EVALUATION						
TRIAL						
ADOPTION						
LOYALTY						

3. For each area distribute a total of 100 % down the steps in the buying decision according to how much influence that key marketing activity has on each stage in the process:

Step	PR	AD	SM	Etc.	Etc.	Etc.
AWARENESS	30 %	45 %	30 %			
INTEREST	20 %	30 %	30 %			
EVALUATION	10 %	0 %	10 %			
TRIAL	5 %	0 %	5 %			
ADOPTION	15 %	5 %	5 %			
LOYALTY	20 %	20 %	20 %			

4. Now, add in a column alongside each key marketing activity to show the spending on that area.

Step	PR	£	AD	£	SM	£
AWARENESS	30 %		45 %		30 %	
INTEREST	20 %		30 %		30 %	
EVALUATION	10 %		0 %		10 %	
TRIAL	5 %		0 %		5 %	
ADOPTION	15 %		5 %		5 %	
LOYALTY	20 %		20 %		20 %	

5. Split the total amount by the percentage you've attributed to each step.

For example, where the whole PR budget is £1200, the advertising budget is £3000 and the social media budget is £720 (there would be more areas of spend on a real marketing budget):

Step	PR	£1200	AD	£3000	SM	£720
AWARENESS	30%	£360	45%	£1350	30%	£216
INTEREST	20%	£240	30%	£900	30%	£216
EVALUATION	10%	£120	0%	£0	10%	£72
TRIAL	5%	£60	0%	£0	5%	£36
ADOPTION	15%	£180	5%	£150	5%	£36
LOYALTY	20%	£240	20%	£600	20%	£144

6. Then output your spend as a bar chart.

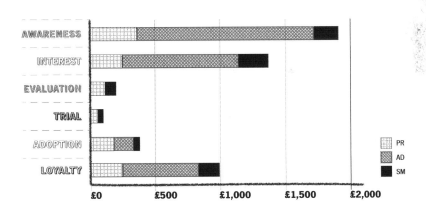

This exercise gives you a powerful tool for both designing marketing programmes and allocating your spend. You're not aiming for an even split, and there's no right or wrong shape to a marketing budget. It will vary depending on the complexity and maturity of your offering. As some guidance, there are typically three highly effective budget shapes I've encountered that can be mapped against the considered purchase continuum.

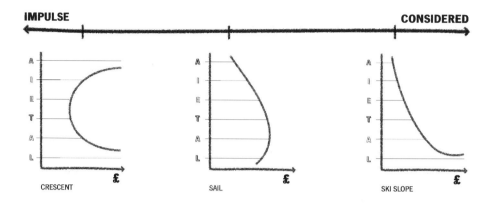

The Crescent: If your business model needs a high number of relatively low value sales, you'll typically need to keep the Taps running and work hard to generate multiple repeat purchases from existing customers. This is often most true in product or transactional businesses.

The Sail: Where you need a steady flow of medium value sales, and then enter into a one-to-one relationship with someone, it's often getting over that first purchase hurdle that takes the most effort. This might be a consultancy or business services company.

The Ski Slope: This is especially true of low volume, high value, sales. Particularly where there's a mix of product and service. Large IT systems design, implementation and servicing are an example of where this budget shape is often seen.

Your budget shape will also depend on how well established your offering is. It stands to reason that if nobody knows about you, you'll need to spend more on generating awareness and explaining what's on offer. For more established offerings, you can often reduce your spend at the top end of the process because your offer is well understood, redirecting this to maintaining and growing your income and referral value of existing customers.

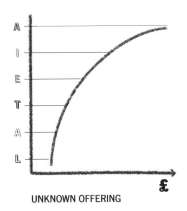

UNKNOWN OFFERING

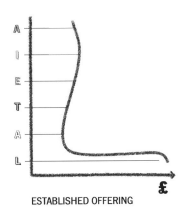

ESTABLISHED OFFERING

If you have a range of offerings, it may be useful to do this exercise against each of your main products and services. The aim of this is to know where you are putting your money against the buying decision so that you can ask yourself if the split is right to support your objectives. This gives you a powerful visual snapshot of any areas of particularly high or low spend.

Neither is in itself a problem, it just acts as a flag to review what you're doing in that area to make sure you have your mix right. You can use this chart, or charts, to help you plan your mix of marketing techniques, ensuring that you have every task supported.

> *This gives you a powerful visual snapshot of any areas of particularly high or low spend.*

Use this chart and planning tool to explain or justify the marketing activity plan you are recommending to your management team.

It can also be used to track any changes in focus over the year. This serves to highlight any likely peaks or troughs in new business as the impact of the spend comes down stream later on.

Use this chart as part of your monthly Board report to show where the emphasis of marketing spend is located and highlight the likely impact on sales later in the year.

The subjectivity here is in how much impact different techniques have at different stages.

This may look highly scientific, but it is important to remember that it is only a visual representation of a subjective view. The subjectivity here is in how much impact different techniques have at different stages. As you've gone through your planning using the Watertight Marketing principles you should have selected an appropriate marketing tool or technique for each task, giving you a good sense of which marketing has an impact where. Whilst this locates the main task on which each activity has an impact, this planning technique allows you to show the more nuanced view of a tool or technique having a level of impact at multiple stages.

If you want to add some rigour or increased objectivity to this, there are a few ways to decide on how much influence a given technique has on each step. You can:

- Run a workshop with key people from sales, marketing and service to agree an apportionment.

- Conduct surveys or focus groups with customers to get them to assess what they saw and responded to at each stage. (This can be tricky, as people often post-rationalise decision making, meaning that emotional stimuli are downplayed).

- A best guess – this is honestly a good starting point.

- A combination of all of the above.

It might be that you start by using your judgement, and then seek to firm it up with evidence and feedback over time.

WORKED EXAMPLE: VA-VOOM!

The VA-Voom! founders were happy to use a 'best guess' approach to this, and worked through the process based on the costs they'd put together for their ongoing 12-month marketing activity plan. They output the following budget shape

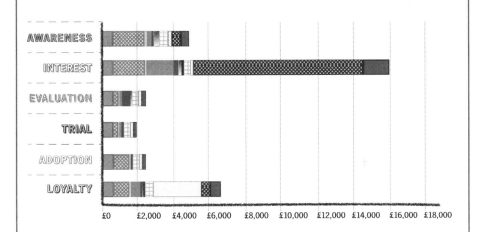

They had expected to see roughly sail-shaped budget, so they were surprised to see the Interest area of their plan seemingly overweighed and the middle part of their process less well supported. On looking at this they found that it was the inclusion of a full price book in their direct mail piece that was adding the heavy costs at this stage, where other areas were mainly supported with digital materials that were made once and used repeatedly. They were comfortable with the shape of the budget, but found it useful for sanity checking the plan they had put together.

To reap the rewards of the Awareness Equation and really create triangulation in your market, you need to commit to an ongoing level of marketing activity. So, once you have the shape for your budget in mind, you need to work out your baseline level of spend. With appropriate allowances for seasonality, the aim is to maintain the shape across the year so that you always have the whole journey supported. It's only when you achieve this that you'll move from sales yo-yo results to steady and growing sales results.

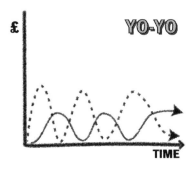

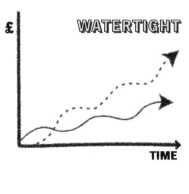

MARKETING ACTIVITY

SALES RESULTS

Which brings us to budgeting. To set a realistic budget, you'll need to understand your maintenance costs and prepare three versions of your activity plan.

In your workbook

- What shape is your marketing budget?

Your ABC Budget

Marketing maintenance costs need to be factored in from day one. Take a look at all of the ongoing commitments you have for marketing activities or technologies, and make sure that these have been budgeted for. These are likely to include such things as:

- Web hosting fees

- Domain name renewals

- Upgrades and patches to web technologies

- Stock replenishment of core marketing materials

- Some premium directory listings you may have invested in

- Memberships of marketing organisations that give you access to best practice advice.

I'd also recommend that you make a reasonable ongoing allowance for things that crop up in all businesses. For example:

- Attending conferences and workshops on new techniques

- Ad hoc design or copy support across the year

- An allowance for imagery that you may need for blog articles and the like.

Once you've worked out your ongoing marketing maintenance budget, you can move on to establishing what you have to spend on activity that directly supports your sales revenues. For this, you need to develop an ABC Budget.

There are always basic and luxury versions of any marketing technique, as well as something in between. What you're looking for here is a gold (A), silver (B), and bronze (C) version of each of the activities you've selected for each of the six marketing tasks.

Let's take PR as an example. On your C Budget, you could buy a book on the subject and put aside a little time each week to do it yourself. Your B Budget might allow you to appoint a PR expert to work on your business for a set number of days each month. And, an A Budget might be upping that expert time and adding in original research from which to generate news coverage. For case studies, the C Budget might allow for a simple write-up on your website, the B Budget could add a short case study video with your client, and the A Budget might stretch to co-hosting a seminar with your client where you present the case study in detail.

Work out a minimum monthly amount that your business can comfortably afford, and base the middle of your three options, your B Budget, on this. Whatever level you go for, you need to maintain the ideal shape you've worked out above, as this ensures that you're covering all six of the marketing tasks adequately.

Having gone through this process, I'd encourage you to commit to the B Budget – knowing that you've got your buying decision bases covered by adhering to your budget shape. You also know what you would step up or down should market conditions demand it.

Adding together your maintenance costs and your B Budget gives you the baseline marketing costs for the year.

In your workbook

- ABC ideas list

- Marketing maintenance list

Your contingency budget

There's nothing more predictable in business than the fact that things will crop up that you can't anticipate. But, just because you don't know exactly what they'll be, does not mean that you can't be prepared for them. You can do this by setting aside a contingency budget and having checkpoints for stepping up or down on your ABC Budget established above. A contingency budget is as important, if not more, for unexpected opportunities as it is for unforeseen problems.

> *Just because you don't know exactly what they'll be, does not mean that you can't be prepared for them.*

There are often moments of heightened awareness of a given issue. If your business is responsive, you can jump into action to make the most of these. This is known as an Issues Jump, in which the following sorts of things might happen that give you a perfect chance to grab the limelight:

- A news story breaks that powerfully illustrates the need for your products

- A competitor goes under or experiences a crisis of some kind

- A new event or publication is launched that is perfect for your market

- A big sporting or cultural event that's captured the public imagination.

Of course, there are also potentially negative scenarios that you may want some cash to put towards should they arise. This is called Crisis Communications and it is needed in these types of events:

- Some sort of reputational damage to your business

- A sudden loss of a big client or reduction in spend from a key market

- A new competitor comes into frame.

I'd recommend that you put together a vanilla template plan for an Issues Jump campaign, and a Crisis Communications package, and put aside the cost of each. These things happen to someone's business every day. If it's yours and you have no pot to go to, you either have to stand frustrated on the sidelines – or raid your baseline budget, jeopardising your pipeline later in the year.

If your budget runs across the calendar year, and you come to October / November having not spent this money, it can be usefully put towards innovative seasonal campaigns or hospitality at the end of the year. These can be really powerful. So, whether you maximise an opportunity, minimise a problem, or do something exciting at the end of the year, this contingency budget will not go wasted.

 Online games featuring seasonal characters, like elves at Christmas or bunny rabbits in the Spring, can be good fun and get people engaged.

Even if neither of these scenarios plays out, all businesses need a level of flexibility in their financial management. Marketing seems to be the natural go-to budget when a business needs to reign in costs, or even splash some cash. In a situation where a saving needs to be found, many will arbitrarily cut an activity of broadly the amount that needs saving – which can often leave a gaping hole in the buying journey that does not become apparent until some months later as the buying timeline takes its course. Conversely, in a situation where some additional cash becomes available, an ill-considered one-off activity (like an ad campaign, big event, or sponsorship) is often undertaken – which can sometimes overweigh the Awareness stage of the buying decision leading to a peak in demand that can be tricky to manage. Or, more often, simply has no real benefit because the subsequent stepping stones have not been built in. This is the equivalent of running an expensive Tap down the drain.

> *Marketing seems to be the natural go-to budget when a business needs to reign in costs, or even splash some cash.*

To avoid this in your business, you need to have that ABC Budget to hand. If you've established a sensible time horizon in which to assess marketing effectiveness, you can use that as a timeframe to review your level of spend. Assuming you've managed to spend at the B Budget level, you already have your step up, and step down, in mind. So, at these checkpoints, or in response to changing market conditions, you can see whether you're on, above, or below target – factor in affordability – and quickly adjust your spending without leaving a hole in your plan.

Taking time to plan your marketing activity and budget in this way will put you well ahead of your competition, both in terms of the robustness of your activities and the speed in which you can respond to a changing situation.

WORKED EXAMPLE: VA-VOOM!

A fully worked Watertight Marketing budget for VA-Voom! is available to download from **watertightmarketing.com**

In your workbook

- Issues jump checklist

- Crisis communications checklist

- Seasonal ideas

Key points

- Make sure you have a marketing activity or tool to support each marketing task.

- Establish the influence each investment has across the whole process.

- For each activity, work out three levels of spend at which it could be delivered.

- Commit to a baseline level of activity across the whole process.

- Establish time horizons and checkpoints to review your spending.

- Monitor your spend across the whole process.

- Make sensible allowances for predictable ad hoc spending.

- Set a contingency budget to cover Crisis Communications and an Issues Jump with fall back spending plans if those urgent situations don't arise.

Further reading:

- **Barez-Brown, C. (2006)** *How to Have Kick-Ass Ideas: Get Curious, Get Adventurous, Get Creative,* **HarperElement**

- **Blick, D. (2008)** *Powerful Marketing on a Shoestring Budget: For Small Businesses,* **Authorhouse**

Mindful measurement

Having a steady queue of people wanting to buy your stuff... now, that's the dream! And, if you apply Watertight Marketing, that's what you'll achieve. In fact, if you really nail it, you won't have to do much 'selling' at all. What you need from your measurement is information that tangibly helps you make decisions about your marketing that keep you on track to the sales results you want.

Three universal lessons

Measuring marketing effectiveness has become its own academic discipline in recent years, and a whole software industry seems to have sprung up to meet the need of businesses to understand whether or not the marketing that they are spending money on is actually turning into profit at the end of the day. The thing about all the technical tools, and academic theories, is that you still need to know which to use, and when.

I could write a whole book on this alone, instead I'm going to pick out the three universal lessons I've learned in regard to measurement from across the hundreds of companies I've encountered in my marketing career. From one man bands to global enterprises, I've observed that marketing measurement is most useful when:

- You make sure you're measuring over the right timeframe.

- You know the difference between an indicator and a real outcome.

- You don't measure the magic out of everything.

Your time horizons

Because considered purchases happen over a series of steps, they also happen over a period of time. So, if you've undertaken an activity that supports step 1 in a 6-step process, you will only know whether it's really worked when enough time has elapsed for someone to have gone through all six. So, if you run an Awareness campaign of some kind, you can't immediately expect to see a difference on your sales figures. You need to work out for your business, or for different offerings within your business, what timeframe is reasonable to measure within. For a fast moving eCommerce business, you may well send an email offer in the morning

> *If you run an Awareness campaign of some kind, you can't immediately expect to see a difference on your sales figures.*

and be dispatching product that afternoon. But, for a complex consultancy business – a speaker gig to raise Awareness – may not turn into paying business for up to six months later. You need to make sure that your marketing measurement is tied to your buyers' timeframes, not your internal business review points. Measuring these things quarterly, for example, might completely skew your perception of how successful the activity was.

Let's imagine that the speaker slot was part of a sponsorship package that cost £10k, from which your salespeople started a number of conversations. From this, a real sales opportunity emerged a few months down the line, a proposal a few months after that, and a signed £100k deal a few months on still. Measuring the ROI on that £10k at the end of the quarter in which the event took place will give you a false sense of poor performance. Getting your review points wrong can actually lead to stopping highly effective activities, because if you measure too soon, you only get half the story. Indeed, in many businesses it's exactly these shortened time horizons that lead to an effect that I call Tactic Burn. It's easy to spot. A business will try something, think that it doesn't work, trash it and try something else. I'm all for innovation and solid 'test and learn' – but 'try and trash' is not that. It's exhausting and a serious drain of money and energy.

The scenario goes something like this: a business owner gets chatting to a friend who does a bit of marketing and casually suggests that Twitter might be a good tool to raise some Awareness. Being a proactive and driven sort, back at his desk he sets up Twitter and emails his sales team to also start using it. They get busy sending out shouty sales messages, and lo and behold it's a complete non-starter. Another common one I've seen is having a panicked look at the sales pipeline, leading to getting a telesales team to hit the phones. They do so, with no gentle offer to draw people in, and funnily enough they get more phones slammed down

Tactic Burn – an exhausting process of leaping from one marketing technique to another hoping to find a silver bullet.

on them than interested buyers. The effect is two-fold; firstly the money spent on the technique is wasted, and secondly the business owner in question writes off that technique altogether with a sense of 'tried that, didn't work'. And, there we have it – Tactic Burn – an exhausting process of leaping from one marketing technique to another hoping to find a silver bullet. If you've worked on your Funnels before turning the Taps on, and you review your results in an appropriate time horizon you reduce the chances of this happening in your business.

It's worth noting that handing over money, i.e. becoming a customer, probably isn't the time horizon we're talking about. It's actually when they've paid you enough money to cover their own cost of acquisition and set-up. If you see customer acquisition as the end of this journey, but your business suffers from a high level of customer defection before you've met a payback threshold, then you could unwittingly be throwing good money down the drain. If you extend your time horizon, you can start to see which marketing activities or sources generate you the customers that stick. It could just be that a campaign that appears on the surface to be highly successful, because it's resulting in lots of new sign-ups, might actually be generating the type of people who cancel early. This is exactly what we observed in the KashFlow case study in chapter four.

Choosing meaningful times for measurement is essential. But, this doesn't mean that you shouldn't find a way of knowing sooner whether the activity is likely to turn out to be successful. This is where the distinction between an *indicator* and an *outcome* is so important.

WORKED EXAMPLE: VA-VOOM!

VA-Voom! mapped out a 16-week journey from initial Awareness to being loyal client making excellent use of a virtual assistant contract. This allowed time for people to go through the whole process, supported by key marketing tools, complete a trial and then receive six weeks of welcome communications. Therefore, this was the timeframe over which they expect to see real sales results.

Interesting, but what does it tell you?

Marketers have an infuriating habit of presenting piles of statistics, as if in and of themselves they mean something. There is a dizzying array of marketing metrics a business could review, from open rates, click-throughs, bounce rates, page views, dwell time, mentions, likes, pins, etc. All of these may constitute stepping stones. An email click-through rate, for example, tells you that someone read an email and went to a web page. It doesn't tell you that these were the right people, or that they read the web page, or that they went any further. Presenting such metrics as if they are real results is like using a thermometer to tell you what tomorrow's weather will be. What's missing here is a predictive element. At its most stark, I would argue that for a marketing metric to be worth knowing, it needs to give you an indication that people are moving towards buying something. There are other uses of various stats, like highlighting areas for design improvement, determining the best timing for an activity, or the effectiveness of one creative route over another, for example. But, at a business level, what you're looking for is a way of visualising the *volume* and *movement* through the buying journey, and then tying that to an ultimate financial *outcome*.

These are the three key things to build into your marketing metrics:

- **Volume:** Key performance indicators (KPIs) for each step

- **Movement:** Progression from one step to the next

- **Outcome:** Return on investment over the whole journey.

The easiest of these is the *volume*, which is really just working out suitable metrics that indicate when people are at each step in your process and counting them. The thermometer analogy is a good one for this type of metric. Tracking *movement* is much trickier, but is extremely useful as over time it can become predictive and give you a valuable planning tool. With measuring the financial *outcome*, the key is to be comprehensive in establishing the total spend on a new customer, and establishing an appropriate timeline over which to measure the ultimate return.

Choosing indicative metrics (KPIs)

By looking at the different steps in the journey, and mapping the techniques that you use for each, you can start to see what to measure to understand the volume of people who might currently be at each given stage. The following table gives an example, but is by no means exhaustive.

Their step	Likely technique	Possible metric
AWARENESS	• Public relations	• Reach of coverage
	• Social media	• Likes, Followers, Connections
	• Direct mail	• Send volume
	• Outbound telemarketing	• Calls connected
	• Search marketing	• Site visitors from search
	• Email newsletter	• Subscribers
INTEREST	• Blogging	• Blog visits, time on page
	• Social media	• @mentions, RTs, Shares
	• Direct mail	• Response rate
	• Outbound telemarketing	• Request for info
	• Web marketing	• Page visits, time on site
	• Email newsletter	• Open rates, Clicks

Their step	Likely technique	Possible metric
EVALUATION	• Case studies • Product pages • Online events • Offline events • Outbound telemarketing	• Page visits, downloads, requests • Page visits, downloads, requests • Registrations, attendees • Registrations, attendees • Meetings secured
TRIAL	• Free trial • Online product demos • Personal selling	• People in trial • Registrations, attendees • Meeting attended, opportunities
ADOPTION	• Discounts, promotions • Personal selling	• Redemptions • Proposals submitted, conversion
LOYALTY	• On-boarding process • Email newsletter • Online events • Satisfaction tracking • Social media	• Retention passed X timeframe • Open rates, Clicks, unsubscribes • Registrations, attendees • Satisfaction scores • Followers, engagement

The aim here is to work out the things you can count that indicate that someone is at a given stage of the buying decision.

WORKED EXAMPLE: VA-VOOM!

Whilst a number of forms of measurement are used to help them plan and refine their marketing activity, the metrics that form part of the VA-Voom! snapshot report are:

Their step	Key techniques	KPIs
AWARENESS	• Public relations • Social media	• Website visits • Social media connections
INTEREST	• Blogging • Social media • Direct mail • Email newsletter	• Blog visits more than 3 minutes • Social media engagements • Responses • Subscribers

EVALUATION	• Time Saver Analyser	• Interactions
	• Case studies	• Case study page visits more than 2-minutes
	• Paper PDF	• Paper downloads
	• Web seminar	• Webinar registrations
TRIAL	• One Month Trial and Audit	• People in trial
ADOPTION	• Monthly contracts	• Contracts secured
LOYALTY	• On-boarding process	• Retention passed 6 weeks
	• Email newsletter	• Open rates
	• Satisfaction tracking	• Satisfaction scores
	• Social media	• Client connections

Visualising progression

As we've said, really effective marketing is to move someone from one step to the next. So, knowing whether or not this is happening is essential. And, it is the key to making the metrics above meaningful and genuinely useful in regard to business planning. There is no point in getting people to open an email, if they then go no further.

Over time, you should start to see a pattern in the percentage of people who take each step.

If you've mapped marketing materials to different stages of the process, it's entirely appropriate to measure engagement with those different materials as an indication of movement from one stage to the next. Over time, you should start to see a pattern in the percentage of people who take each step. You're aiming to establish an average conversion rate between the six steps. This allows you to plan, and track, your marketing effectiveness.

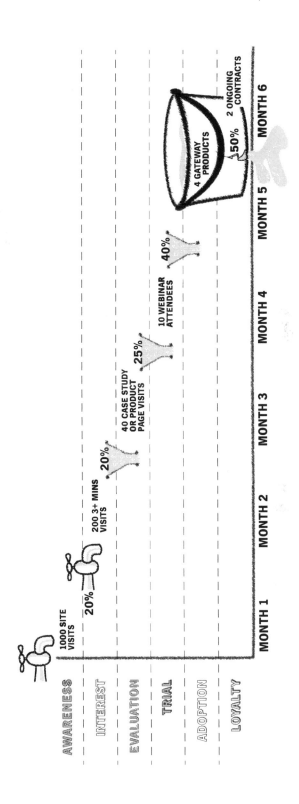

In the charted example above, to achieve two new long-term customers per month, the company needs to generate 1000 website visits each month, and there is a six-month time lag. So, assuming that the Funnels were working effectively, and they were aiming for 3 new customers per month to meet their target, generating 1500 site visits should enable this target to be met within six months. The indicative metrics at each later stages would allow them to assess whether they were on track. Any variation from the results they were expecting could be used to act as a flag to review the effectiveness of the tools they're using at that stage, the skills of the people using them, or the appropriateness of the Awareness activity being undertaken.

Once you've established your conversion rates, you can work back up through the process to set monthly targets against each indicative metric.

Once you've established your conversion rates, you can work back up through the process to set monthly targets against each indicative metric. Armed with an understanding of customer value, and with revenue targets in mind, you can then work out the sales and marketing goals you'll need to reach at each stage in the process to hit that target.

Depending on your product and service mix, you may have a slightly different pattern for different types of offering. For example, purchasing a downloadable template could happen within six minutes, whilst the consulting services you offer might take six weeks to convert. You'll need to establish this for each of your key offerings.

Use Google Analytics to set goals based on actions on your website to visualise progression through your website.

The tricky aspect of this is working out accurate conversion rates. How you do this will depend very much on your business, the data you have, and how long you've been tracking it.

The following are all very sensible ways of setting these conversion rates, increasing in robustness as you go down the list:

- In the absence of data or if your offer or business is new, set rates that you all think are reasonable and achievable.

- Reach a 'best guess' based on your previous experience and that of your sales and marketing team.

- Perform a retrospective analysis of sales and marketing data.

- Build a predictive model from a large enough test activity amongst a representative sample of your audience.

WORKED EXAMPLE: VA-VOOM!

As we saw earlier, VA-Voom! set the target of upping their monthly personal subscriptions from 160 customers paying an average of £350 per month, to 225 customers paying an average of £425 per month. The target is to take annual revenue against this offering from £672,000 to £1,147,500. This meant securing 65 new clients in the next 24 months, which is an average of 2.7 per month (they rounded this up to 3 for their target setting purposes). However, because a number of the things they introduced were completely new, they had no scientific way of setting conversion rates. Historically they knew that they've managed to secure about 1 new contract per month. But, they were not really sure how these people came their way. They did know that about half of the people who actually speak to an assistant about a contract went on to sign up, and about half of those currently made it past six weeks. Extrapolating this, they agreed that reaching their target meant these are the sorts of monthly indicators:

Step	Current	Target
AWARENESS	Unknown	425
		10%
		↓
INTEREST	Unknown	43
		25%
		↓
EVALUATION	Unknown	11
		50%
		↓
TRIAL	4	5
	50%	75%
	↓	↓
ADOPTION	2	4
	50%	75%
	↓	↓
LOYALTY	1	3

What this meant in practice was that they would need 425 opportunities to exist for someone who knows a little about VA-Voom! to find out more, from which they'd want to see 43 instances indicating someone showing some Interest each month across blog visits, social media interactions and active email newsletter subscribers. Of these, 11 would go on to take the *Time Saver Analyser,* download the paper or attend the web seminar. 5 of those would take up the one-month Trial and *Time Saver Audit*. 4 would then sign up for a monthly contract, and 3 would get past the first six weeks.

In your workbook

- What's your time horizon?

- Indicator or outcome?

- Mapping your marketing metrics

- What are your conversion rates?

What constitutes an outcome?

Having established your *volume* and *movement* metrics, you now need to find a way of seeing the full and true financial picture. You're looking to measure your return on investment (ROI). To fully understand this financial *outcome* of your marketing you will need to work out:

- **Your investment:** the full cost of securing a new customer

- **Your return:** the true value of a customer.

Start by working out your investment. For this you'll need to know the cost of customer acquisition and the cost of set-up.

You've seen through all the chapters so far that people move through a journey. What this means from a financial perspective is that they pick up costs along the way. Where many businesses fall down in terms of the completeness of their understanding of the cost of marketing is by only counting the cost of the initial activity that sourced the potential buyer, rather than the cost of taking them through the whole journey. You need to

> *You need to remember in this that a new customer needs to carry the cost of the people who didn't buy.*

remember in this that a new customer needs to carry the cost of the people who didn't buy. For example, if you sent a direct mail piece to 200 people, and 4 people eventually signed up, the cost of the full 200 mailings would need to be distributed across those four customers. Using your Watertight Marketing budget in which you've established the proportion of your marketing budget you've spent supporting each step, and your conversion rates, you can work out an average cost per step in the process. From this, you can establish the average cost of the marketing activity used to support a sale. You do this by dividing the spend across the whole six-step buying decision by the number of customers secured.

For each key product or service, work out your average costs of all the marketing activities used to secure a new customer.

Another potential blind spot in terms of understanding the full cost of securing a new customer is making sensible allowances for how much it costs the business to get the customer set up. For example:

- Adding them to your systems

- Initial set-up meetings or phone calls

- Typical early support calls.

For each key product or service, work out your average set-up costs for a new customer.

When you add these two costs (acquisition and set-up) together you'll see the total investment. This is the full cost to secure a new customer for your business. You can do this calculation retrospectively to establish actual costs or use your projected numbers to establish a target costs.

If you want to get really forensic about costs, you can also attribute the cost of the people and a proportion of overheads involved in the process of customer acquisition and set-up.

WORKED EXAMPLE: VA-VOOM!

The 12-month B Budget for VA-Voom! came in at just over £33,000. When they started the initiative they had 160 contracted clients. The target was to increase this to 225 within 24 months. So, for the year this budget pertained, they were looking to secure 33 new contracted clients. This meant that their target cost of customer acquisition was approximately £1000. They worked out that getting a client set-up on their system cost them about £250 per client. To secure their 33 new *loyal* customers, they'd need to set-up 44 clients as 25% were forecast to cancel before six weeks. So, covering the costs of the clients who don't make the transition, the set-up costs are averaged at £333 per client. So, the full cost to secure a new customer for VA-Voom! is £1333.

This is the I in ROI. You then need to work out your return. But, measuring return, that is the true value of a customer, is also a nuanced business. At its simplest, you can look at their first purchase and see that as the return. So, if a customer has just signed-up and paid you £100, and it cost you £50 to win their business then your ROI is 2:1. However, this can give a distorted view.

Depending on the complexity of your business, and making allowances for ongoing cost to serve, you might need to take time to understand two further concepts:

- **Payback period:** how long it takes for you to break even on a customer.

- **Lifetime value:** how much an average customer is worth to your business over the whole duration of their relationship with you.

Payback is understanding when the customer has covered what you paid out to secure them in the first place. If you look just at the first month, for example, the initial outlay is likely to look completely out of line. Knowing the full cost to secure a new customer and roughly how much money the new customer will bring in over a given

If cash flow is a critical requirement in your business, speedy payback will be essential.

timeframe means that you know how long you need to keep them to break even on the money you've spent. It's only after this point that they start making you a profit. If cash flow is a critical requirement in your business, speedy payback will be essential. So, if it costs you an average £300 to secure a new customer, and they make you £100 per month, you will hit payback at month three. This is when your business typically starts to make a profit.

WORKED EXAMPLE: VA-VOOM!

The target average monthly spend for the contracted customers was £350, equivalent to 8 hours at £42. With ongoing costs to serve of roughly £20 per hour, £160 per month, the monthly profit for VA-Voom! stands at £190 per month. By dividing the full cost to secure a customer (£1333) by the monthly return they achieve (£190) they worked out that it would take just over seven months to reach payback on a new Loyal customer.

Lifetime value is how much you will make from a customer for the whole time that they remain a customer of yours. This is what they are really worth to your business. Understanding this may mean that you are willing to spend more on acquiring a customer in the first place, forgoing speed of profitability in return for ongoing revenue and long-term sustainability. Let's imagine that the average customer above on whom you make £100 per month

Armed with this information you might decide to invest more heavily in high quality marketing to secure more of this kind of customer.

typically stays with your business for three years. This means that they're actually worth £3600 to your business (£100 x 12mths x 3yrs = £3600). Armed with this information you might decide to invest more heavily in high quality marketing to secure more of this kind of customer.

WORKED EXAMPLE: VA-VOOM!

Looking back through their records, VA-Voom! found that of those clients who made it past six weeks, the average length of the relationship stood at two and a half years (30 months). This meant that the lifetime value of a Loyal VA-Voom! client is £5700 (monthly return of £190 x 30 months).

When you've worked out the four key items above you can set clear financial marketing objectives, to include:

- The average cost of customer acquisition.

- The payback period on the marketing spend.

- The average lifetime value of the customers secured.

In your workbook

- What's the full cost to secure a customer?

- What's the lifetime value of a customer?

- What's the payback period?

- Your financial marketing objectives

Your starting point

Getting your measurement mapped across the buying decision is powerful for planning ahead as we've seen – but what is also extremely useful is that you now have a clear order of play for addressing each area to increase your profits. And, that's bottom up – the opposite to the way that most businesses approach it. The seemingly obvious way to increase profits is to pour more into the top, but it can actually be much more effective to tweak up through the process, so that every penny you spend on those expensive Taps has an increased chance of turning into profitable long-term customers.

Let's imagine a company with two regional offices is currently securing an average of 2 new customers per month on an ongoing contract, and they've set a target of increasing this to 3 per month. The conversion rates across the buying process are currently the same in both regions. Both regional managers achieve the target. However, one increases marketing costs by £500 per month, whilst the other spends £500 upfront and adds less ongoing cost. The difference? Their starting point. The manager in Region One simply expands their monthly direct mail campaign to go to an additional 500 people. This is a top down approach that seeks to run the Taps a little harder. Meanwhile the manager in Region Two takes a bottom up approach where a single investment in a triggered set of emails across their two-week Welcome Window stems a hole in their Bucket and means that 25 % more of their Trialists go on to sign up for the ongoing contract. Region One's approach is logical, but the gain is in volume without an improvement in margin and therefore has less impact on ongoing profits. Region Two is the far smarter way forward. The improvement in margin means that the effect will be compounded month on month. What Region Two has achieved is a real improvement in long-term sales results.

Their step	Cost per interaction	Current Performance	Region One	Region Two
AWARENESS	£1	1000 10% ↓	1500 10% ↓	1000 10% ↓
INTEREST	£2	100 30% ↓	150 30% ↓	100 30% ↓
EVALUATION	£10	30 27% ↓	45 27% ↓	30 27% ↓
TRIAL	£50	8 50% ↓	12 50% ↓	8 50% ↓
ADOPTION	£250	4 50% ↓	6 50% ↓	4 75% ↓
LOYALTY	£1000	2	3	3
Total spend		**£4900**	**£7350**	**£5900**
Cost per loyal customer		**£2450**	**£2450**	**£1967**

The other major benefit to addressing it this way around, is that you're able to reinvest the early returns in higher quality tools and techniques upstream. This should then further improve your results. In the scenario above, if the profit from

This becomes a virtuous circle, because the effect is compounded as you move up.

the extra customer each month in Region Two was then reinvested to extend the monthly direct mail to reach 1500 people, they would see a leap to four new customers per month. The impact would be even greater still if they worked up incrementally improving the conversion rates at each step from the bottom to the top. This becomes a virtuous circle, because the effect is compounded as you move up.

CASE STUDY: KashFlow

The KashFlow team are particularly focussed on the conversion of people taking their free trial. For Duane Jackson, Chief Executive, addressing the Adoption phase of the process first makes complete sense. He comments, "Assuming you convert 20 % of trialists to paying customers and you increase the 'visitor to trial' by 2 % – you get 0.4 % more customers. Whereas a 2 % improvement in trial-to-paying results in 2 % more customers. The other benefit of optimising the end of the funnel is that it has a knock-back effect on the beginning. If you convert a higher rate of trialists, then you're willing to pay more to acquire a trialist in the first place."

A bottom up approach also has the effect of meaning the improvements pay for themselves along the way. In a small business, where cash flow is often a key challenge, this can make the difference between actually doing this stuff or not. And, we haven't accounted for the benefit to your Commercial Karma in meeting or exceeding more people's expectations, thereby generating positive word of mouth and increased referrals. So, it really is worth fixing your Bucket, and lining up your Funnels *before* turning the Taps on or up.

If you're not seeing the final sales figures you need, address the process bottom up for faster payback and better long-term results.

In your workbook

- How much impact could you have?

Don't measure out the value

Measuring your marketing, and responding to it, is key to making a decent return on your investment. But, it's also worth being alert to the fact ROI as a key metric can put your business on a downward spiral if you don't balance it out with a commitment to certain values and quality standards.

Value your values

The nature of the ROI equation is that the less you spend, and more you charge, the better the ratio. What this can lead you into is constantly reducing your spend. Looking to shave off spend at each step can significantly up your profitability. But, you need to make sure that these incremental reductions in spend don't add up to an overall degradation in quality.

And, given that there's a time lag to knowing the real market response to what you put out there, you may not find out if you've overstepped the mark that stops people wanting what you have.

> *You need to make sure that these incremental reductions in spend don't add up to an overall degradation in quality.*

Let's take Apple, makers of the Mac, iPhone, etc. as an example. Anyone who has ever bought an Apple product can't have failed to notice the exquisite packaging. It's beautiful, right down the sticker that reads 'lovingly packed in California'. Now, a simple review of their ROI could lead to a recommendation to cut back on what must be a pretty significant cost – both in terms of materials to create such high quality packaging, and in the expensive American labour to pack it. But, it's exactly this sort of attention to detail that has helped Apple to build the brand and reputation that keeps customers coming back for more and paying what might seem to be significantly inflated prices.

You need to establish your quality standards, and stick to them. Remember your Commercial Karma. Every time a customer or potential customer comes into contact with your business you create an impression. Work out what impression you want that to be, and always maintain or improve it. People don't mind when quality improves, but they hate it when it reduces.

Being slavish to an ever-improving ROI can lead you into a trap of drilling holes into the side of your own Bucket.

Work out those things you do that are representative of your brand and your values, and protect them from any cuts in spending.

Good now, or better later?

Don't spend months agonising about the metrics you use for planning.

For many businesses, particularly smaller businesses, doing something you know is pretty good is always better than standing around until you know it's perfect. I'm a firm believer in getting solid marketing metrics in place. But, I'm not one for getting paralysed by it.

If you spend too long working out exactly what your conversion rates are, or should be, without actually getting on with fixing your leaks, you are necessarily losing money. So, don't spend months agonising about the metrics you use for planning. Having something in place you think is reasonable, and then refining it with more robust data over time, is a perfectly sensible approach.

Don't let establishing your metrics hold you back from getting on with the common sense activities laid out so far.

Cost of entry

You also need to make some allowance for things you can't measure. There genuinely are some marketing activities that just need to be there, and that are almost impossible to measure. To a certain extent, there's some marketing that is just the price of doing business – the stuff you need to stay on people's radar.

CASE STUDY: Mubaloo

In terms of knowing what works, Mark Mason, Chief Executive at app developers Mubaloo, is clear that there's a cumulative effect. He continues, "I've never been able to put a precise pounds value on winning a big award, for example, but I know that when this is added to our other activity it comes together to be more than the sum of its parts." Mubaloo grew from £0 to £2.5m turnover in three years.

If you think back to the idea of triangulation, it's often the third instance to which people respond. This is what shows up in your reports as the source for that individual. But, had it not been for the earlier two exposures, the third touch would not have triggered a response. Thinking also of the zigzag way in which people make their way through a buying decision, you may be maintaining a person's Awareness for a couple of years before they finally do something that shows up as an action you can measure.

You certainly shouldn't justify your entire marketing plan on this basis. But, you should be mindful of it. This is where the commitment to your Baseline Budget is essential. It's exactly this 'little and often' approach to marketing that builds the background levels of Awareness and goodwill that you need to really step up those sales results.

> *You certainly shouldn't justify your entire marketing plan on this basis. But, you should be mindful of it.*

In your workbook

- Save it or spend it?
- Spending cuts sanity checklist

At the risk of writing a chapter on management accounting, what you're aiming for is marketing measurement that's mindful of the impact that its use has on the decisions you make and in total alignment with your company's ultimate financial goals.

Key points

- Choose indicators to show engagement at each stage of the process.

- Work out average conversion rates from one step to the next.

- Understand the financial outcome your business needs.

- Understand all the costs of customer acquisition.

- Address improvements in the process from the bottom up.

- Have a commitment to core values and standards.

- Be mindful of things that cannot be measured.

Your lifelong marketing habit

Marketing is like exercise. It's best when it's a fun and healthy lifetime habit, rather than a chore or short-lived fad. Throughout this book we've seen how powerful it can be to make marketing an underpinning skill in your business. But, if it's still looking like an uphill struggle, let's look at it again from two angles – firstly all those reasons for doing it, and secondly breaking it down into something manageable.

Making a step change in the way you market your business means addressing those Four Foundation Leaks head on. To really make the leap that puts your business on the path to long-term, predictable, profits, you'll need to make marketing part of everything you do.

Leak #14 – The wrong kind of work – You can only become the best at, and most recognised supplier of, something if you know exactly what that something is. You'll need to identify:

- Your passion – *what do you love doing?*

Leak #15 – Unused marketing muscles – You need to commit to a regular and balanced set of activities to keep your company marketing fit. For this, you'll need to address:

- Your overall fitness – *are you in the right shape?*

- Your regular regime – *are you maintaining a routine?*

Leak #16 – No familiarity to work from – You need to make sure that you're never starting from a blank sheet of paper. This means thinking about:

- Your platform – *are you doing enough to make a difference?*

Leak #17 – Expensive exhaustion – With any ongoing commitment, you'll only stick at it if you steel your nerve and make it fun. Take time to consider:

- Your vision – *can you see the horizon and the next step?*

If some of these questions seem familiar, it's probably because you've thought about them before. Perhaps in January when you bought that gym membership or promised to shift a few excess pounds... because, marketing is like fitness. And, like getting fit, it's pretty addictive, and great fun, when you get the hang of it!

Marketing is like fitness

I don't imagine that anyone reading this book hasn't at some point thought about, started, or even already done some of what's been recommended. It's stepping it up and keeping at it that that separates the best companies from the rest.

It's stepping it up and keeping at it that that separates the best companies from the rest.

When talking to small business owners and managing directors about marketing, I often hear:

- They start a new marketing activity with real vigour, but then lose interest.

- The results of their marketing are never quite as good or as fast as they'd hoped.

- Marketing is an area of the business that they get time for sporadically, in between all their other commitments.

- They live in hope, albeit vain hope, that one day someone will show them 'the answer' to sustainable sales results.

To my ears, this sounds an awful lot like talking to many people I know about fitness. Perhaps some of this rings a bell?

- Starting many a year with the determination to go for a run every day, but slipping back into sloth-like habits within weeks.

- Abject disappointment that it's not actually possible to drop a dress size in the week before a beach holiday.

- Exercise always slipping down the list after work and family commitments.

- Thinking that getting fit is just a matter of finding the *right* diet, or the *right* exercise class.

- Wishing it was possible to feel and look great without having to try.

The thing about dipping in and out of a fitness regime is that it doesn't work. To get fit, the 'little and often' approach is far more effective than big bursts followed by extended periods of inactivity. The same is true in marketing – I'd often actually prefer businesses to spend less overall on marketing if they did so in a sustained way, than see huge peaks and troughs in activity. I'm sure a GP would prefer it if every patient did a little exercise every day, rather than the boom and bust of un-sustained good resolutions.

> *The thing about dipping in and out of a fitness regime is that it doesn't work.*

Here are ten ways in which achieving Watertight Marketing is like getting, and *staying*, fit:

1. It is hard to change the habits of a lifetime.

2. If things have gone to seed, you'll need to put in some groundwork.

3. A regular, structured, approach is best.

4. It's even better if you integrate a little into everything you do.

5. Some people are absolute fanatics, but most do fine with smaller changes.

6. There are lots of people out there promising quick fixes that don't really work.

7. It takes a little while to see the results.

8. To get the best all-over results you need to vary the techniques you use.

9. There are people who can help.

10. Your company will look great, feel great and, it's fun.

Leak #14 – The wrong kind of work

Your passion – what do you love doing?

Powerful marketing is based on great products and services. Great products and services are based on being genuinely useful. What this often means in practice is continually having conversations with people about their issues, and how they might be resolved. It's going to get repetitive. And, whilst it may be new for the people you talk to, you will have heard it all before. So, if you and your team don't honestly enjoy helping people with whatever it is you do, you will never keep the conversation going. If you're bored by answering the same questions, or uninterested in what people do with your answers, your marketing will fail.

If you don't love what your business does, you'll keep getting pulled in other directions and never find the passion and commitment you need to step off the roller coaster. Where on a fitness drive your vision might be that little black party dress, with your business the marketing vision has to be more about your customers

> *You need to be excited about what you can make possible for them.*

than yourself. You need to be excited about what you can make possible for *them*. Take some time to really look at what you do. Is it brilliant? Do other people agree with you? Do you love seeing the results of people using your stuff? Do you love helping people achieve those results?

If you can't answer *yes* to all of those questions, stop, and think again. If you can, brilliant. Now, stay true to it, and stop doing anything that distracts you from it.

Leak #15 – Unused marketing muscles

Your overall fitness – are you in the right shape?

You can't get fully fit and truly toned by doing just one form of exercise continually. You need a mix. The precise mix will depend very much on your particular areas of weakness. To support an entire buying decision you need to choose a range of marketing activities, tools and materials. Using the Thirteen Touchpoint Leaks as your guide, you should now have an idea of where you need to work a little harder. And, if marketing is something that's been a little neglected in your business, or you've just not looked at it from end to end before, then you'll need to put some hours in upfront. You'll need to commit to an initial investment of time and money to get the leaks fixed. Then you'll be in the right shape to start a regular routine.

> *Using the Thirteen Touchpoint Leaks as your guide, you should now have an idea of where you need to work a little harder.*

It's worth saying here that there's a lot you can do under your own steam, but if you've not done something before, or you find that your business has numerous leaks, you probably need someone to show you how. Making marketing up as you go along is as dangerous to your business health as it would be to walk into a gym and jump on the first bit of kit that caught your eye. And, just as it's not wise to take health advice from unqualified quacks, you will need to choose your marketing advisers carefully. Ideally, you should build an ongoing relationship with a marketing advisor who will come to know your business intimately so they can quickly see if you're going off track and point you back in the right direction.

Your regular regime – are you maintaining a routine?

Once you've got yourself in shape, you'll want to keep it up. Stopping at this point will waste much of the effort put in to getting here. It would be like hitting your goal weight and then slipping back to old habits and piling the pounds back on. The nature of the Awareness Equation, triangulation and the time it takes to run through a considered purchase necessarily mean that results take time. Keep the image of the yo-yo sales results chart in your mind. This is habit you're breaking. It's the steadier, and growing, chart you're aiming for. So, once you have yourself in good shape, and you've chosen a set of ongoing activities to support the whole buying decision, I suggest that you commit to a full year of doing them to really see a step change. If you're not ready for an ongoing commitment to marketing, don't waste your time doing the groundwork.

> *It would be like hitting your goal weight and then slipping back to old habits and piling the pounds back on.*

It's worth having a little expert input here too. Whilst you're busy running your business and getting to grips with your new marketing muscles, an expert marketer will be busy keeping up to date with the latest innovations. And, there will be innovations. I can't tell you what the new Twitter, Pinterest or Instagram might be, or which of the current crazes will soon be seen as yesterday's fad. I can tell you that new marketing techniques *will* come and go, and squeezing more from what you already do is almost always possible. I can also tell you with almost 100 per cent certainty that you will save time and money if you take advice from people who've already tried and tested the new and the old, rather than trying to work it all out from scratch.

> *I can't tell you what the new Twitter, Pinterest or Instagram might be, or which of the current crazes will soon be seen as yesterday's fad.*

Leak #16 – No familiarity to work from

Your platform – are you doing enough to make a difference?

If you've got yourself in shape, and you've made the commitment to see it through, you need to be sure that you have the basics covered. This is probably what I'd equate to a healthy diet in my fitness analogy. Now, you need to get active. The level of activity you commit to will have a direct correlation with the results you achieve. And, there's a level below which it's barely worth doing. For any of the techniques we've been through to work for your business, you'll need to be doing enough of all of them to get a bank of familiarity in place. This is your platform for growth. This is a bit like core strength. Doing one press-up a day won't help. Doing 5, then 8, then 10, then 20... will steadily build you up. Make sure that when you get started with Watertight Marketing you're doing enough to make a difference. Then once you're seeing the benefit, step it up a level. That ABC Budget will be enormously helpful in allowing you to ramp up when you get into the swing of things.

> *There's a level below which it's barely worth doing.*

Leak #17 – Expensive exhaustion

Your vision – can you see the horizon and the next step?

If you were starting a fitness drive and said you were going to run 10km per day from day one, you'd be almost guaranteed to fail. The same is true of Watertight Marketing. You need to think about it at two levels. Have the long-term vision in mind – that toned exemplar of a business with enviable sales results all on an upward curve and an army of raving fans telling the world how you changed their lives – but set yourself stepping stone targets to getting there. And, you need to prepare yourself for times when you'd rather curl up under your duvet. Your market might take a dive. Your business might lose a key member of the team. If – or should I say *when* – tough things happen, it will be hard to motivate yourself to keep going, keep spending, keep the marketing machine running. But, you must. A marathon champion doesn't skip a training run because it's raining. And, the very best businesses don't stop marketing when the chips are down. And, of course, you'll have your ABC Budget in hand, so you'll be able to cut back if you need to without leaving gaps. Just think... if you can keep going in a storm, imagine how amazing you'll be when the sun shines.

If you can keep going in a storm, imagine how amazing you'll be when the sun shines.

In your workbook

- What's your vision?
- 2-week planning checklist
- 12-week project plan
- 12-month project plan

Remember...

Get Watertight Marketing in place for your business and really show the world what you can do. If you get it right:

- You will do more of the right kind of work.

- You will break the cycle of feast and famine.

- You will have more control over your business growth.

- You will attract the very best people to work in your business.

- You will build a positive momentum that pulls you forward.

- Your business will be scalable.

- Your business will be salable, and...

- You will have helped tens, hundreds or thousands of people to solve that problem they were having!

Further reading:

- **Barlow, N. M. (2006)** *Re-Think: How to Think Differently,* **Capstone Press**

- **Heppell, M. (2004) 2nd ed.** *How to Be Brilliant,* **Pearson**

- **Johnson, S. (1998)** *Who Moved My Cheese?* **Vermillion**

- **Meaden, D. (2009)** *Common Sense Rules: What You Really Need to Know About Business,* **Random House**

- *The Mind Gym: Wake Up Your Mind* **(2005), Time Warner**

SUMMARY OF PART FOUR

Marketing that truly supports long-term sales results is marketing that is mapped to the way that real people really buy things. This means having at least one marketing tool or technique for every step in that process. How much emphasis you put on each will depend on your specific offering, and your business objectives. The key is to appropriately cover every step, and to keep doing so whatever your budget and whatever new challenges come your way. To know that this investment is giving you a return, you'll need to have a way of seeing the volume and movement through the buying decision. This will enable you to plan and prepare your business to deliver brilliantly. Achieving this might mean using muscles you've not flexed before, so it can take time to build core strength and see visible results. But, when you do, you'll really mean business.

On your marks.
Get set.
Go!

About the Author

Bryony Thomas is a proven marketing professional, with a passion for helping ambitious entrepreneurs make their marketing pay through her speaking, writing and hands-on consultancy. She has a distinctive no-nonsense style that makes you sit up and take notice, and a real talent for unravelling how marketing delivers sales results. Bryony lives and works in Bristol in the UK.

Having occupied senior roles on both sides of the client/agency relationship, Bryony has a unique perspective on the marketing industry that enables her clients to get the most from it.

She started her marketing career at just 19, working in telephone fundraising for ActionAid, whilst also studying at the University of Bristol. Following her first marketing role in charity fundraising in the late nineties, Bryony's formative years were spent with multi award-winning business-to-business marketing agency, Mason Zimbler. Whilst there, the agency supported her in securing her Chartered Institute of Marketing Diploma – a course that she has since tutored. By 24, she was responsible for the agency's largest account running pan-European campaigns with the likes of IBM, Dell and HP. She went on to lead the pitch team that secured the multi-million pound Microsoft account, which the agency retains to this day. Working freelance for clients including Lloyds TSB, whilst securing an MBA with distinction, Bryony undertook an award-winning strategic customer management project for database specialists ClarityBlue, where she subsequently became Director of Marketing. She's proud to have played a key role in raising the profile of this 200-person business as part of a strategy that saw the company sell to Experian for £85 million in 2006. At just 28, Bryony secured the position of divisional Director of Marketing for the FTSE 100 company, reporting directly to the Board.

In 2008, driven by an entrepreneurial spirit and a passion for helping small businesses realise big ideas, she set up a consultancy business, Clear Thought, and has since built a reputation as a compelling business speaker and writer. 2013 sees the launch of her new business – Watertight Marketing – so, watch this space!

Book Bryony as a speaker

Bryony Thomas is an energetic public speaker who shows businesses and entrepreneurs how to make marketing pay. Her speaking style is no-nonsense and direct. She doesn't shy away from tough subjects, and makes highly effective use of memorable analogies to make her ideas stick. Bryony has a real skill for adapting her content to suit the needs of her audience, both through thorough preparation, and by being extremely quick-witted and responsive to the audience in front of her.

bryonythomas.com
@bryonythomas

Find a Watertight Marketing consultant

Are you looking for a reputable strategic marketing consultant to be your guide through putting a Watertight Marketing operation in place for your business? You will find details of accredited Watertight Marketing consultants on the Watertight Marketing website. These people have been carefully selected to ensure that they can be trusted to support your small business through the step change you're looking for.

Become a Watertight Marketing consultant

Are you a marketing consultant with extensive strategic consulting experience looking to set yourself apart and work with ambitious growing businesses? Take a look at the criteria for Watertight Marketing accreditation and membership to see if you could join the elite group of no-nonsense marketing experts.

watertightmarketing.com
facebook.com/watertightmarketing
@watertightmkg

BRAIN FOOD

If you're a marketing student, or academically-minded, you may wish to read up on the theories and concepts that have contributed to my thinking. In the list below you'll find phrases and ideas related to key areas of content of the book. Many are commonly used marketing terms, most of which are based on original concepts from marketing academics.

1. Models of Adoption

2. High Involvement Purchases

3. Customer Journey Mapping and Customer Touchpoints

4. Marketing Orientation

5. Decision-Making Unit

6. Marketing Exposure

7. Supplier Selection

8. Cognitive Development, Psychology of Buying

9. Logic and Emotion (You can go right back to Aristotle's Rhetoric for discussion of Cognos, Logos and Pathos. There are also lots of scientific texts on left and right brain functions.)

10. Source Credibility

11. Influencer Marketing

12. Networking and Network Marketing

13. Word of Mouth (WOM)

14. Abundance Mentality

15. Marketing Myopia

16. Product Proposition

17. Key Account Management and Pareto Principle

18. Customer Orientation

19. Loyalty Incentive

20. Post Purchase Reassurance

21. Operational Performance

22. Brand Identity

23. Inclusive Language and Tone of Voice

24. C-Suite Marketing, CxO Campaigns, (part of Influencer Marketing)

25. Affiliate Marketing

26. Halo Effect

27. Triangulation

28. Selective Attention, Selective Distortion and Selective Retention

29. Single-Minded Proposition

30. Brand Monitoring

31. Balanced Scorecard

32. Activity Based Costing

Useful academic text books

Most of the ideas above can be found discussed in depth in the following marketing and management text books:

- Fill, C. (2006) *Simply Marketing Communications,* Prentice Hall

- Hooley, G., Saunders, J. and Piercy, N. (2004) 3rd ed. *Marketing Strategy and Competitive Positioning,* Prentice Hall

- Kotler, P. (2000) *Marketing Management,* Prentice Hall

- Payne, A., Martin, C., Clark, M. and Peck, H. (1995) *Relationship Marketing for Competitive Advantage,* Butterworth Heinmann

- Palmer, R., Cockton, J.and Cooper, G (2007) *Managing Marketing: Marketing Success Through Good Management Practice* Elsevier

- Slack, N., Chambers, S. and Johnston, R. (2004) 4th ed. *Operations Management,* Prentice Hall

If you can't find what you're looking for in these books, the phrases above will probably give you a useful starting point for Internet research.

INDEX

Bold page numbers indicate figures.

C

D

E

F

The Thirteen Touchpoints Leak Checklist

Step	Leak	Think about
AWARENESS BE THERE	**13** NO EMOTIONAL IMPACT	*Why does it matter?* • Emotional hook (problem)
	12 WHAT	*What are you talking about?* • The right kind of work • One theme, three messages • Name and strap line
	11 WHO	*Are you mentioned by other people?* • Word of mouth • Conversation starters
	10 WHEN	*Have you got your timing right?* • Selectivity • Seasonality • Scheduling
	9 WHERE	*Are you everywhere they turn?* • Triangulation
	8 HOW	*Can they digest as they want to?* • Format selection
INTEREST BE RELEVANT	**7** INFORMATION OVERLOAD	*Is it worth five minutes?* • Invitation information

Step	Leak	Think about
EVALUATION BE PROVEN	**6** NO PROOF	*What do people say about you?* • Endorsements • Affiliates • Referrals *Where's the evidence?* • Facts and figures • Case studies • Guarantee
TRIAL BE HELPFUL	**5** NO CRITICAL APPROVAL	*Who can say no?* • Reaching third parties • Equip for internal selling
	4 NO GATEWAY	*Is there a tiered path to payment?* • Product ladder • No-commitment trial
ADOPTION BE FRIENDLY	**3** NO EMOTIONAL CONNECTION	*What kind of people are you?* Visual identity • Tone of voice • The personal touch
	2 POOR ON-BOARDING	*Do they get what they expected?* • Welcome Window • Welcome Pack • New customer communications
LOYALTY BE CONSISTENT	**1** FORGOTTEN CUSTOMERS	*Do you stay in touch?* • Customer communications *Are you available to help?* • Three-level customer support • Customer satisfaction tracking • Proactive service communication

Key Conceptual Imagery

You can download these images
for use with permission in your own
presentations, talks and articles from
watertightmarketing.com/gallery

The Buying Decision Continuum

IMPULSE BUY

LOW RISK

CONSIDERED PURCHASE

HIGH RISK

The Watertight Marketing Framework

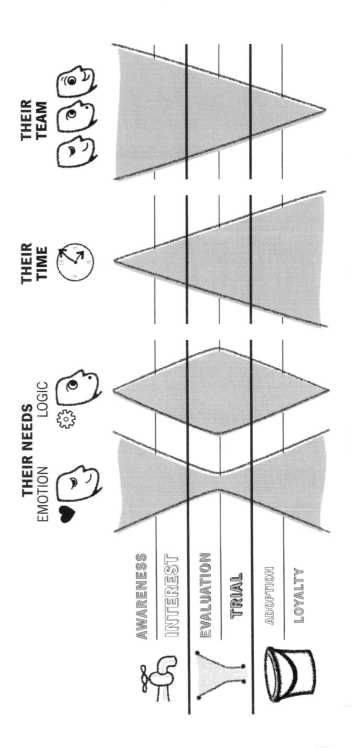

Watertight Messaging

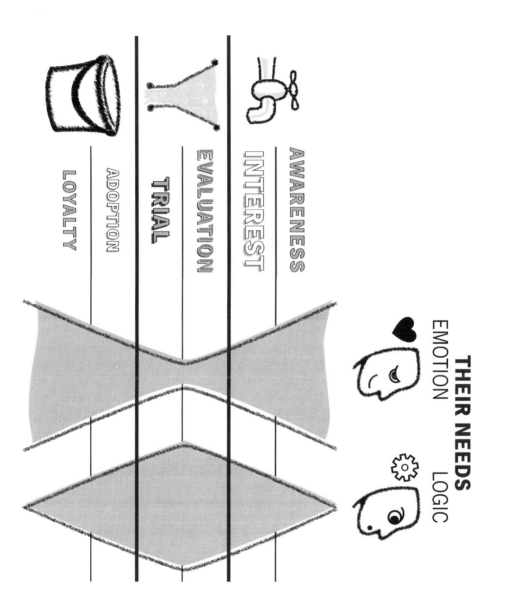

Watertight Timing

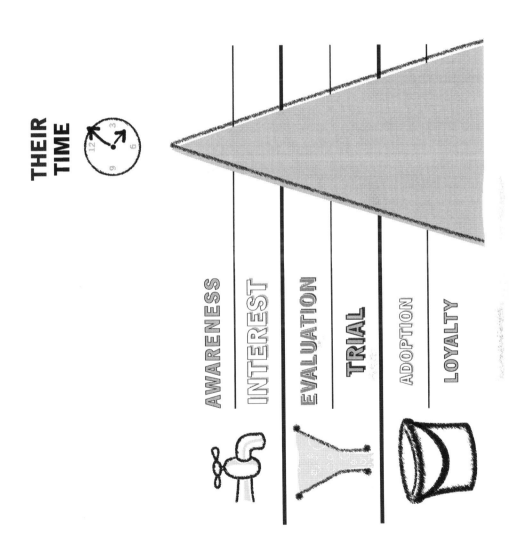

Watertight Audiences

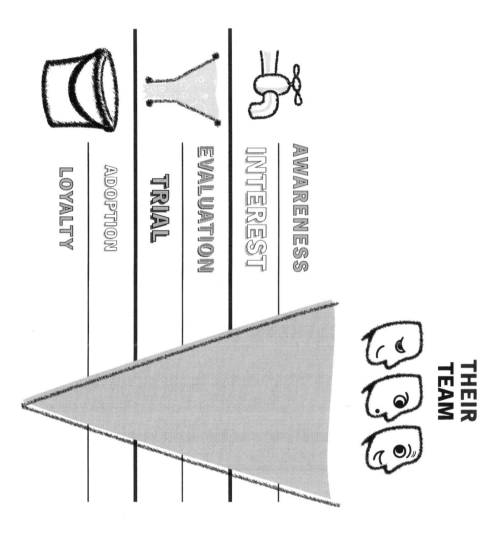

The Thirteen Touchpoint Leaks

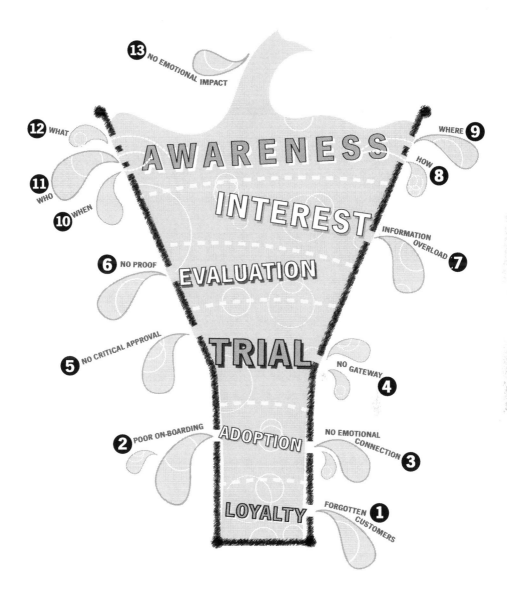

ZigZag Timing

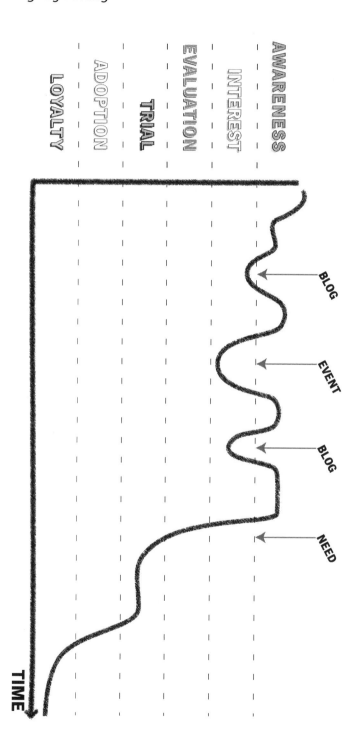

Watertight Budget Shapes

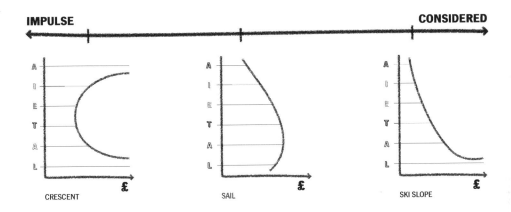

IMPULSE   **CONSIDERED**

CRESCENT   SAIL   SKI SLOPE

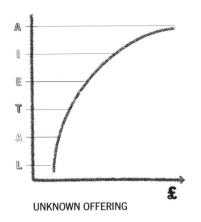

UNKNOWN OFFERING

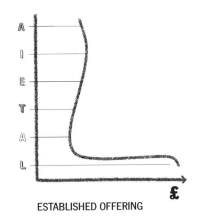

ESTABLISHED OFFERING

Yo-Yo Marketing

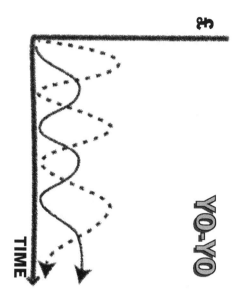

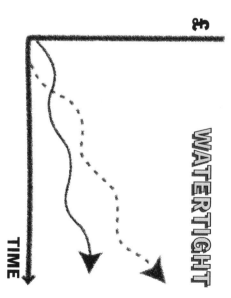

Conversion Rates

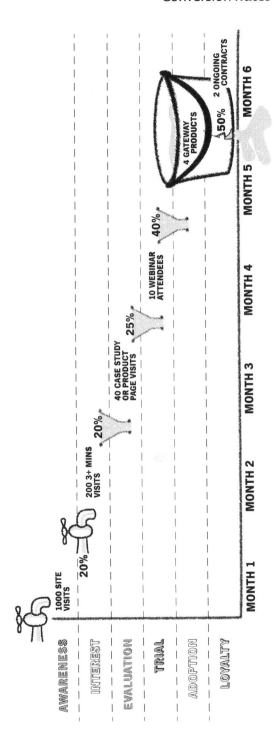

AWARENESS — 1000 SITE VISITS — 20%

INTEREST — 200 3+ MINS VISITS — 20%

EVALUATION — 40 CASE STUDY OR PRODUCT PAGE VISITS — 25%

TRIAL — 10 WEBINAR ATTENDEES — 40%

ADOPTION — 4 GATEWAY PRODUCTS — 50%

LOYALTY — 2 ONGOING CONTRACTS

MONTH 1 | MONTH 2 | MONTH 3 | MONTH 4 | MONTH 5 | MONTH 6

twitter.com/watertightmkg

facebook.com/WatertightMarketing

pinterest.com/bryonythomas/watertight-marketing/

www.watertightmarketing.com

Printed in Great Britain
by Amazon